WHAT'S IT ALL ABOUT?

Eleven years as a missionary in the South American jungles . . . twice married, twice widowed . . . mother, author, teacher, Christian intellectual and questing woman. Elisabeth Elliot has witnessed the miracle of God's grace in her gifted, giving and often tragic life. Yet troubles and triumphs alike have only strengthened the faith of this singular woman. In TWELVE BASKETS OF CRUMBS she shares her perceptions of the meanings of the events in her turbulent past. In these essays she speaks out on family, marriage, motherhood, widowhood . . . on liberation, how to be free, memories, boredom, truthtelling, the shock of self-recognition, the generation gap, housework, love, nature, freedom. . . . on discipline, spontaneity, endurance, faith . . . on patience, hope, courage, and women who have accepted the challenge of world missions.

Twelve Baskets of Crumbs

ELISABETH ELLIOT

PILLAR BOOKS  NEW YORK

TWELVE BASKETS OF CRUMBS
A PILLAR BOOK

Published by arrangement with Christian Herald House

Pillar Books edition published April 1977

ISBN: 0-89129-250-0

Library of Congress Catalog Card Number: 75-45855

Printed in the United States of America

PILLAR BOOKS
Pyramid Publications
(Harcourt Brace Jovanovich, Inc.)
757 Third Avenue
New York, New York 10017
U.S.A.

I   OUR LIVES TOGETHER

II   TO LEARN AND TO TEACH

III RISK AND SERVICE

Foreword

Many years ago photographer Cornell Capa explained to me that the camera is the extension of the eye. If I was to learn to take pictures I must learn first of all to see things, and to capture with my camera the things I saw in the way that I saw them. I watched Mr. Capa at work, and discovered that he chose some very odd angles from which to shoot. His angle of vision, then, determined how he communicated his subject.

"Photograph things you care about," he told me, and I started with my little daughter and the Indians I loved. I hoped that the people who looked at the pictures would see what I had seen in them and would know the way I felt about them.

One of the tribes had been called savage, and not without good reason. But as I learned to know them and watched them laugh and hunt and cook and care for their children, I began to understand what our common humanity meant—not merely that they were "as good as" we who called ourselves civilized, or that we were "just as bad," though both facts were obvious. It brought clearly to my attention the equality of our human condition. All of us, I saw (and tried to show in the photographs), were created by the same God, all of us were broken by the same Fall, and all of us might be redeemed by the same Grace.

Returning to the United States after eleven years as a missionary, I saw everything in the light of that exotic experience. How could I help it? My perspective had been altered. North American culture looked different to me because of where I had stood. There was a different light on it.

An Indian woman from one of those tribes where I worked was taken to New York City to see the sights. How would this citadel of the civilized world look to a woman reared in the forest, learned in the planting of manioc, the making of clay pottery, the smoking of wild game?

She surveyed the panorama spread out before her—harbor, ocean liners, tugboats, bridges. She said nothing. She peered over the parapet into the canyon of the street where people and cars swarmed and crawled. Still she said nothing. At last something caught her imagination—a splotch of white on the ledge in front of her.

"What bird did this?" she asked.

Nobody, I thought when I heard the story, nobody but Dayuma would have seen that, and seen nothing else worth mentioning. Man's vehicles and structures were of mild interest (Indians build canoes and houses, too, of course, and why should Dayuma be impressed with the differences in scale and design?), but that some bird had actually made it to the top of this building in this sterile treeless place called for comment. Who Dayuma was, what her life's experience had been, determined what she saw.

If a book of essays deals with more than a single subject nothing can give it unity except unity of vision. This book is a potpourri, but the observations were made by one person. Another person, from another vantage point, with a different range of experience, would have seen it all differently.

As an ex-missionary, I saw missionary meetings differently than I had before I went to the jungle. I had a new appreciation for what had been done, for example, by "One of Those Nineteenth Century Missionaries" who always seem to come in for such harsh criticism. When I was asked to tell, in writing and public speaking, the story of my work I wrestled with the question of honesty, with the "generation gap," with the emotionalism of my readers and hearers and with my own (often very different) feelings. The essays "Truth Telling," "Two Ladies' Meetings," "Return to Order," "Is There a Hero in the House?," "Speaking and Thinking: First the Latter and Then the Former," and some others were written as it were from "the other side" of the podium and typewriter.

"M is for a Merry Heart" is about my mother, but I wrote it not only as her daughter, but from the viewpoint of a mother who herself has a daughter.

Some of the pieces (the only obvious one would be "Twelve Baskets of Crumbs") came out of the experience of marriage, some written while I was married, some after I was widowed, so the perspective changes. Those that deal with suffering came from vicarious as well as from personal experience.

Acutely, at times painfully, aware of the limitations of my vision and ability, I see myself as a comic figure and ask, almost every time I tackle a piece of writing (and certainly every time I reach that dead blank in the middle of the job when I simply cannot *get on* with it), "whatever gave me the idea I could do this?" But I am heartened by a command given to great writers, the biblical prophets, millennia ago. They were men of widely differing experience, background, education, and imagination, but, divinely chosen to write the books which would become holy scripture, they were given the same direction: *"Write what you see."*

Though what I have seen—as a missionary, as a writer or speaker or mother or wife or widow or teacher—is neither inspired nor apocalyptic, I try not to be disobedient to the prophets' command. Here is the assortment. These are things I have seen.

9

I

OUR LIVES TOGETHER

Tyrannies and Victories

THERE ARE MANY things people want to be liberated from, many kinds of tyranny from which we would like to escape, but one of the inescapable ones is the tyranny of change. (I didn't make up that idea. I got it from Paul, reading the Phillips' translation of Romans 8:20–21.)

Most of us are ambivalent about change. We say, "Let's do this for a change," or "I've simply got to have a change," and in the next breath we moan, "Oh dear, how things have changed! They're just not the same anymore." Lots of people do things purely for the sake of doing something different. And one of the ironies (tyrannies are full of ironies) is that things don't necessarily turn out to be all that fresh and original after all.

A group of young intellectuals got together on a farm near Boston and began growing their own fruits and vegetables, milking cows and building rustic houses in which they could live together simply and study without the distractions of the Establishment. They were fed up with hustle and bustle, and just wanted to be themselves. There was a lot of sitting around on floors and stairs, a lot of discussion and reading and dancing under the stars, some trips to Boston for lectures or concerts.

They all had a great interest in Eastern religions, and some of them were followers of a strong-minded woman who thought it was high time members of her sex were liberated and allowed to speak their minds about a few things. Most of the people in this commune believed in nonviolence. Peace was what they were after. They liked long hair and long beards. Spontaneity was a great word in their vocabulary and "doing things in crowds" was their idea of the good life.

But the blue the men wore was not jeans. It was tunics. Some wore something called "plain brown holland." The lectures they went to were not on racism but on anti-slavery. The commune I am talking about was Brook Farm, founded more than a hundred years ago in an effort to find a whole new direction.

I was thinking about that effort, wondering how many times in history it has been repeated, when my aunt happened to give me a box of old family papers. I love old stuff like that and can hardly keep away from it. Here were personal letters from as far back as 1817, old pictures, diaries, house plans and newspaper clippings. I found myself reading everything, even the advertisements on the backs of the clippings.

A column from *The New York Journal of Commerce*, written by my great-great uncle and dated July 19, 1864, has this list of things for sale on the back of it: *Common shippers oak timber plank; Sycamore Lumber for Tobacco Boxes; Patent Portable Sectional Houses* (I had just read about modules last week and thought it was quite a change in building technique); *Black Walnut library shelves; Tar-Thick, Thin, and Rope; 150 bbls. Spirits Turpentine in prime shipping order; Cudbear* (I had to look that up—a purple dye made from lichens); *500 bags Singapore pepper; 60 kegs choice Dairy Butter; 75 bales New Orleans Mess* (porridge? I'm not sure); *French and Dutch madder* (the dictionary says a red dye); and a lot of other things like *smoked unbagged hams* (were they better than bagged ones?), *fire crackers, carb ammonia, re-reeled Canton silk, and whortleberries.*

14

It sounded to me like a list of things to do without. But take any similar list from the advertising of 1976. A magazine that came last week has Oriental porcelain, a lion skin, a $725 crystal koala and some fifteen-inch potted fig trees. More things I can deny myself.

But there we are again—a lot of effort and study goes on in the advertising business year in and year out. They've improved the presentation of ads, certainly—all those colored pictures (those gorgeous sweeps of lawn, those intimate, elegant living rooms), the catchy, understated text, the catch questions ("Is seepage disturbing your loved ones?")—but they're still up to the same trick, to make me think I ought to feel a need where I felt none.

One entirely predictable thing about life is that there will be changes. Some of the changes are themselves fairly predictable—birth, puberty, marriage, parenthood, suffering, old age, death. We rejoice and recoil when we think about these things. If only there were some safe place where we could halt the progression exactly where we want it.

One morning recently I read in the paper about a prisoner who had just been released after sixteen years and asked to remain in prison. He was denied the privilege, so down he went to a tavern, phoned the police to report a robbery and waited patiently until he was arrested as the thief. Back in his cell he explained that he felt at home there, that he wanted to finish an art course he had started in prison and that, furthermore, things had changed a lot in the outside world, and he didn't like it.

I wondered if he saw the cartoon that appeared in *The New Yorker* that same week, showing a guard complaining through the bars to a man in the striped suit, saying, "Take me now. I'll go home on a packed bus, find the wife in tears over some crack a neighbor made, listen to a depressing newscast, bawl the kid out for a lousy report card, eat an underdone casserole, hassle over what TV show we're going to watch, find somebody else has taken the last beer in the icebox and finally settle into a fitful sleep punctured by a neighbor's hi-fi."

The prisoner in the cartoon is slumped down on a bench, hands clasped behind his head, listening to all of this and looking very pleased. People have different ideas of freedom, and they get out of one kind of tyranny and fall into another. The man in the news story wanted the kind of freedom which order, security and sameness afford. Iron bars didn't bother him as much as change.

I understand that man. I don't like change very much. I am not always moving the furniture around. I don't want any "bright new taste surprises" for breakfast. I want the sofa where it was yesterday and the black coffee just the way I always make it.

It was reassuring to me to learn that C. S. Lewis also liked monotony and routine. Urged time and again to journey abroad to lecture, he stayed home and smoked his pipe and lectured where he felt he belonged. He also wrote wonderful things and remained content with familiar surroundings, able to draw on deep inner resources. Andrew Wyeth found enough to paint in two towns in Pennsylvania and Maine.

The ocean can teach us very many things. Change is its essence. It can be counted on ceaselessly to change, and this is the source of its beauty. The waves roll in, sweep the shore, suck out and roll in again. It does this in almost the same way each time, but there is something endlessly fascinating in watching how it happens. The swell and the crest, the break and crash, the glass-green turning to milk-white, the cream, the foam, the bubbles, the thin sheet that slides back so smoothly and disappears so suddenly—who can take his eyes off it? But each change is in perfect harmony with the nature of the ocean.

We need not be always seeking something different, something other, out of mere restlessness. There are enough changes we cannot stop, which are of the essence of this life and are meant to be. They are meant to drive us to God.

The world of creation, said Paul, has, in God's purpose, been given hope. "And the hope is that in the end the whole of created life will be rescued from the tyranny of change and decay, and have its share in that magnificent liberty which can only belong to the children of God."

Among the treasures in that box of old family papers was a series of letters from a great-aunt who was serving as a hostess in a rest house in Virginia during World War I. She was a lady unused to working for a living, but her husband dropped dead one day at the bank where he worked, and she had to find a way to support herself. Soldiers and sailors came to the house, some of them terribly homesick, some of them just back from the front with permanent disabilities. The wives and mothers of men who had been killed sometimes arrived at the door in the middle of the night, having just received the sorrowful news. The great-aunt took care of them all.

Her letters to her brother "Chigsie" (Charles Gallaudet Trumbull) are full of cheerfulness and compassion. She was busy helping others every minute of the day and night; as I read her vivid and often humorous accounts of the daily routine, I remember the background of suffering against which she wrote— her own suffering (she could hardly bear to think of returning to the house where she and her husband

17

Jack had lived) and that of so many others. But doing everyday duties for the sake of others saved her.

People who have themselves experienced both grief and fear know how alike those two things are. They know the restlessness and loss of appetite, the inability to concentrate, the inner silent wail that cannot be muffled, the feeling of being in a great lonely wilderness which both emotions can produce. They are equally disabling, distracting and destructive.

One may cry out in prayer and hear no answer. The heavens are brass. One may search Scripture in vain for some word of release and comfort—there are plenty of such words, but how frequently they seem only to mock us, and a voice whispers: "That's not meant for you. You're taking it out of context" and no such word reaches us.

Faith, we know perfectly well, is what we need. We've simply got to exercise faith. But how to do that? How to exercise anything at such a time? "Pull yourself together!" With what? "Cheer up!" How? "Think positively!" But that is a neater trick than we are up to at the moment. We are actually paralyzed. Fear grips us tightly, grief disables us entirely. We have no heart.

At such a time I have been wonderfully calmed and strengthened by doing some simple duty. Nothing valiant or meritorious or spiritual at all—just something that needed to be done, like a bed to be made or a kitchen floor to be washed, one of those things that will never be noticed if you do it, but will most certainly be noticed if you don't. Sometimes it takes everything you have to get up and do it, but it is surprising how strength comes.

Ezekiel was a man who witnessed many strange things and prophesied great cataclysms and splendor. He told us little about himself, but in the twenty-fourth chapter of his book there is a powerful

18

parenthesis: "The word of the Lord came to me: 'Son of man, behold, I am about to take the delight of your eyes away from you at a stroke; yet you shall not mourn or weep nor shall your tears run down. Sigh, but not aloud; make no mourning for the dead. Bind on your turban, and put your shoes on your feet; do not cover your lips nor eat the bread of mourners.' So I spoke to the people in the morning, and at evening my wife died. And on the next morning I did as was commanded."

God asked more of Ezekiel than any human being would dare to ask, but he knew his man. He was asking him to "put on a front," to act normally, not as a mourner. To put on turban and shoes and eat his usual food—what extraordinary commands to a man who has just lost the delight of his eyes! But Ezekiel had had plenty of practice in obedience and it was not his habit to bridle. "My wife died . . . I did as I was commanded."

It sounds simple. But not easy. It was heroic, certainly. There are other incidents in the Bible where the doing of very ordinary things helped people out of deep trouble. When Paul was sailing as a prisoner to Italy and was about to be wrecked in the Adriatic Sea, everyone on board was terror-stricken, sailors were trying to escape, the soldiers and centurion and captain were all sure they were doomed and paid little attention to Paul's assurances of faith in God. But when he suggested that they eat, and actually took bread himself and gave thanks for it, "then they all were encouraged and ate some food . . . and when they had eaten enough, they lightened the ship, throwing out the wheat into the sea."

Terror had disabled and disoriented them. In their panic they thought only of desperate measures which might have saved a few. But where Paul's faith had

had no effect on them, his common sense—"Let's eat"—restored them to their senses. Then they were able to see clearly what the next thing was to be done. From panic came peace. The result was salvation for everybody.

I never noticed until recently that the beautiful story of the woman with the alabaster box of perfume occurs between the high priests' plot to kill Jesus and Judas' deal with them to betray him. The Son of Man knew exactly what he was going to Jerusalem for. But in the face of those tremendous facts he moved with perfect serenity through each day's activities, walking, talking, sleeping and eating. He even had the grace to sit at supper with his dear friends in Bethany (one of them a leper) and to accept the woman's oblation of love.

He moved on into the Passover with his disciples, taking it as next in order. The Jewish Passover was a feast he had always kept. He would keep it this time, too, as usual. Had we been in his place we would surely have said, "What's the use? Who can go to feast at a time like this?" But our Lord did not halt all activity to brood over what was to come. He was not incapacitated by the fear of suffering, though he well knew that fear. To the question, "What shall I do?" (so often, for us, the cry of despair) he simply answered, "This," and did what lay in his path to do at the moment, trusting himself completely into the hands of his Father. This was how he endured the cross.

We can better imagine the utter paralysis of grief and fear that overcame the disciples of Jesus and the women who loved him in that worst hour when he drooped dead on the cross. No one could think of a thing to do. It was over. God had left. The last shred of hope that God might intervene or that the physician would heal himself had gone. There hung the mutilated corpse, the blood dried by now. But "a good and righteous man" named Joseph from the Jewish town of Arimathea had the presence of mind to think of a few practical things that needed to be done. He went and asked for the body, took it down from the cross, wrapped it in a new linen shroud and laid it in his own new tomb.

Emmi Bonhoeffer writes in *The Auschwitz Trials,* "From the very moment one feels called to act is born the strength to bear whatever horror one will feel or see. In some inexplicable way, terror loses its overwhelming power when it becomes a task that must be faced."

Joseph's action gave the women the courage and vision they needed to see what they, too, might do. I imagine that that darkest of Friday evenings was made endurable for them because they had work to do for Jesus.

They prepared spices for the body. They rested on Saturday, according to Jewish law, and it was, I believe, a peaceful day for them even while they sorrowed because it held the promise of a clearcut task next morning. What a morning it turned out to be! But they would have missed it if they had abandoned their common work and given themselves over to grief.

Thomas Carlyle said, "Doubt of any sort cannot be removed except by action." There is wonderful therapy in getting up and doing something. While you are doing, time passes quickly. Time itself will in some measure heal, and "light arises in the darkness," slowly, it seems, but certainly.

According to a poem, the source of which I have been unable to find (can any reader help?), there is a Saxon legend inscribed in an old English parsonage, *Doe the nexte thynge.* "Do it immediately," says the poem, "Do it with prayer, do it reliantly, casting all care." I know it works. I have been hauled out of the Slough of Despond by those four words. And in the doing of whatever comes next, we are shown what to do after that.

How to Be Free

ISAK DINESEN, the great Danish storyteller, describes two men traveling by dhow to Zanzibar on a full-moon night in 1863. Mira Jama, a much-renowned old man, "the inventions of whose mind have been loved by a hundred tribes," tells a red-haired Englishman "who had been blown about by many winds," that "there are only two courses of thought at all seemly to a person of any intelligence. The one is: What am I to do this next moment?—or tonight, or tomorrow? And the other: What did God mean by creating the world, the sea, and the desert, the horse, the winds, woman, amber, dishes, wine?"

I am captivated by the scene—the warm night, the smooth sea, the creak of the mast and the quiet voices. But beyond that Mira Jama's statement has for me the ring of truth. It touches the foundation of all that the Bible says to us, for it is a book about man's responsibility and God's purposes. But there is a question which alone is regarded as "relevant" (Mira Jama's word "seemly" is a much better word!) to today's generation, one "up with which I can no longer put," a question discussed in schools, churches, clubs and "sensitivity groups" ad nauseam. It is WHO AM I? I protest the endless probing and pulse-taking, the anxious inward examination which assumes that the ego is the place to look for answers, and that the truth which makes us free will somehow be found in "knowing oneself." Can we not call it plain old-fashioned selfishness if we ignore the possibility of responsibility to others and to God as the road to freedom? According to Mira Jama, "a person of any intelligence" would want to be informed not of who he is, but of what is expected of him.

One weekend three things happened to my teen-age daughter Valerie which brought home, more powerfully than any lecture of mine could have done, the tragic delusion of modern youth's quest for identity and freedom. On Friday night her best friend ran away from home. On Saturday night Valerie saw the movie *Easy Rider*. Then on Sunday morning the rector's sermon was on freedom, using *Easy Rider* as an illustration of a misguided pilgrim's progress. Valerie herself saw the relation between these events, and was awed by the "coincidence," to me not less than providential.

Her friend, whom I'll call Becky, had suggested once or twice that she'd like to run away. She had not been happy with her mother, so had decided to try living with her father and stepmother. She didn't like that either. They also expected her to let them know where she was, and come home at reasonable hours. This was a bit much for Becky, who had attended a school in New York where "we never had to worry about things like getting homework done or coming to class on time." She filled Val's and other friends' ears with astonishing tales of things she had experienced, and took a condescending view of people who were not pot smokers. To her, freedom meant doing what she wanted to do. She had not yet acknowledged to herself that she did not know what that was. "Maybe the trouble's inside me," she confided to Val. "But I think it's outside. It's my environment. If I can get away from it all, find out who I am, do my own thing. . . ."

Easy Rider is the story of two young men who do just that. They use money made in selling dope to cut loose from their responsibilities and head for what

24

looks to them like the Holy City—New Orleans, at Mardi Gras time. One of them starts out by discarding his wristwatch. None of the restrictions of time for him! He is free. And off they go, roaring across the great sunlit spaces of the West, the warm peacefulness of the South. Neither of them notices that if it weren't for the Establishment there would be no smooth highway to travel on, no high-powered bikes to carry them.

The rector's sermon pointed out that true freedom is not to be found in throwing off personal responsibility. The man who runs away from the truth will never be a free man, for it is the truth alone, sought within the circle of his commitments, which alone will make him free.

Dietrich Bonhoeffer, a man who epitomized true freedom in his acceptance, for God's sake, of the prison cell and death, wrote: "If you set out to seek freedom, then learn above all things to govern your soul and your senses . . . Only through discipline may a man learn to be free."

Freedom and discipline have come to be regarded as mutually exclusive, when in fact freedom is not at all the opposite, but the final reward of discipline. It is to be bought with a high price, not merely claimed. The world thrills to watch the grace of Peggy Fleming on the ice, or the marvelously controlled speed and strength of a race horse. But the skater and horse are free to perform as they do only because they have been subjected to countless hours of grueling work, rigidly prescribed, faithfully carried out. Men are free to soar into space because they have willingly confined themselves in a tiny capsule designed and produced by highly trained scientists and craftsmen, have meticulously followed instructions and submitted themselves to rules which others defined.

I spent some time living with a jungle tribe whose

style of life looked enviably "free." They wore no clothes, lived in houses without walls, had no idea whatever of authority, paid no taxes, read no books, took no vacations. But they had a well-defined goal. They wanted to stay alive. It was as simple as that. And in a jungle, which can look very hostile indeed to one not accustomed to living there, they had learned to live. They accepted with grace and humor the awful weather, the gnats, the mud, thorns, snakes, steep hills and deep forests which made their lives difficult. They never even spoke of "roughing it." They didn't know anything else. They'd walk for hours with hundred-pound baskets on their backs and when they reached their destination, perhaps in a tropical downpour, they did not so much as say, "Whew!" They knew what was expected of them, and did it as a matter of course. None asked, "Who am I?" They asked only, "What am I to do this next moment?" If it were to hunt or to make poison for darts a man did that, or if it were to go out and clear new planting space a woman did that. Their freedom to live in that jungle depended on a well-defined goal and on their willingness to discipline themselves in order to reach it. No one could "give" them this freedom.

I lived with these footloose people in their "jungle" environment—a nonproductive member of their community—and enjoyed a kind of freedom which even hippies might envy. But I was free only because the Indians worked. My freedom was contingent upon their acceptance of me as a liability and, incidentally, upon my own willingness to confine myself to a forest clearing where all I heard was a foreign language.

So we come back to Mira Jama and Becky and the "Easy Riders," and their search for meaning in life. It can be found only in God's purpose, I believe, in what he originally meant when he made us. "If you are faithful to what I have said, you are truly my disciples (those who are being disciplined)," Jesus said. "And you will know the truth and the truth will set you free."

All That Was Ever Ours

IN HIS beautiful book *For the Life of the World*,
Alexander Schmemann says that time is "the first 'object' of our Christian faith and action. . . . Through
time on the one hand we experience life as a possibility, growth, fulfillment, as a movement toward the future. Through time, on the other hand, all future is
dissolved in death and annihilation. . . . By itself time is
nothing but a line of telegraph poles strung out into the
distance and at some point along the way is our
death."

All my life I have been acutely conscious of time,
having grown up in a family where six o'clock meant
five fifty-five, and because my father was superintendent of the Sunday school we got there as much as an
hour early. In the past ten or fifteen years I have
become more conscious of it, not only for the obvious
reason that when one reaches middle age he knows it's
running out, but also because as a speaker I'm used to
being told how much time I'm allowed (ten minutes,
thirty minutes) and I try to stick to it. (I am agonizingly aware of time when the speaker who precedes me is
cheerfully unaware of it.) I marvel at the program
planners who arrange to have, following an hour and a
half of banqueting, a "short" business meeting, a "few"
acknowledgements (getting the ladies out of the kitchen for a round of applause always takes a long time—
one of them is still wiping her hands on an apron and
won't come, another only peeks around the door with

the sheepish protest, "But I didn't do anything!"), a couple of guitar numbers (is there a short guitar number?), a testimony or two and one of those things we used to call movies which are now, for reasons beyond my understanding, called "multi-media presentations," before the speaker or speakers take the platform. Time doesn't seem to mean much of anything to those planners until the speaker stands up and then they wonder how in the world it got so late and hope most fervently that the speaker will make it short.

But if time is the first object of our faith and actions as Christians we need to learn to redeem it, to say with the psalmist, "My times are in Thy hands," and to realize that it has been once for all transformed. God incarnate entered time. Jesus Christ "suffered under Pontius Pilate," a particular Roman procurator in a particular place at a particular point in history, redeeming us and the world we live in, transforming forever that bleak "line of telegraph poles strung out into the distance." Nothing is meaningless. Nothing, for the Christian, is a dead end. All endings are beginnings.

I need to remember this just now, because the Cottage is about to go on the market. "The Cottage" is a summer place in the White Mountains of New Hampshire, built in 1889 by my great-great uncle and aunt, and the scene of gloriously happy family vacations ever since. It was to me as a child the very vestibule of heaven. We would leave Philadelphia on the night Pullman, the "Bar Harbor Express," and I remember the delirium of joy with which I settled into the berth, my clothes safely stowed in the little hammock, and fell asleep, to be awakened in New Haven by the shifting of the cars as the train was divided into different sections. I would lift the blind and see the brakeman passing with his lantern, watch the baggage trucks rolling by, and try to read in the dim light the thrillingly romantic names on the freight cars in the yards —"Seaboard Airline," "Lackawanna," "Chicago and Northwestern," "Route of the Phoebe Snow," "Atchison, Topeka, and Santa Fe," I remember the jerking of the uncoupling and the satisfying crunch of the coupling, the loud hissing of steam and then the gentle rolling out of the station, the giant engine building up speed until the clickety-click reached the rhythm that once again put me to sleep.

In the morning I woke to see the Connecticut River valley, and it was not long before we pulled into Littleton, were met by my grandfather's Buick and driven the eight miles to the Cottage. My stomach tightened with the joy of that first glimpse of the two brick chimneys, visible as we crossed the Gale River Bridge, and then, as we turned up the driveway, I could see the beloved house, the breakfast table set in the sun on the front quarter of the porch. (The porch ran all the way around the house, which was rectangular, built stockade-style, with six-inch spruce blocks for walls in the lower portion, shingles above.)

The sound of footsteps hurrying from the kitchen on the old boards. The creak of the hinges on the massive door which had a key eight inches long. (It was said that Uncle Will had the big iron lock and key before he built the house, and had to construct a door on a comparable scale.) A race around the porch to see if the little cart we played with was still in its place, to look into the separate cabin which was the kitchen at the back of the porch, a pause to look at the mountains —Lafayette, Artists' Bluff, Bald, Cannon, Kinsman— blue against the sky, always dependably the same, strong, comforting ("So the Lord is round about them that fear Him"), waiting for us to climb them once more. In the living room, the huge fireplace with its three-foot andirons; the green china clock on the mantel, the guns in their niche; the fishing rods cradled in bentwood hooks suspended from the ceiling; the Texas Longhorns, the deer head; the portrait of Uncle Will on the wall; the rocking chairs where Grandpa and Grandma Howard always sat by the heavy writing table which Uncle Will had made with his own hands; the converted kerosene lamps; the little melodion which we used for accompaniment at our Sunday evening hymn sings (the "natives" came to these, including a little old lady who claimed she couldn't sing "half's good's a crow"); the cushioned settee with a lid which lifted to reveal a furry mechanical bear, a black lace parasol, a music box, and a mummified human child's foot, brought from some ancient tomb in Egypt by Uncle Will back when he was scrounging the world for things to put in the then new Metropolitan Museum in New York.

In the back parlor were crumbling leather-bound books, a set of bells, a stereopticon with magic pictures of ice caves and frozen waterfalls, astonishing in the perfection and depth of each gleaming crystal, the glass cases of moths and butterflies which Aunt Annie had lured by stretching a bedsheet in the light of a lantern on the porch at night. And upstairs were books and more books, brightly colored stuffed birds from foreign lands, Aunt Annie's flower press, a vial of attar of roses from a forgotten tomb, and life-sized paintings of improbably large brook trout that Uncle Will had caught, painted and pasted to the door panels. There was the little room with the bird's-eye maple and bamboo furniture where I slept, snuggling down under a feather quilt and listening to the wind in the white pines, the sound of the river flowing over the stones, and there was a poem tacked to the wall, "Sleep sweetly in this quiet room, O thou, whoe'er thou art . . ."

And oh, the smell of the place! Year after year it was the same. Year after year we rushed in and breathed that sweetness—old wood, old leather, old books, the perfume of pine and balsam and wood smoke. There is no accounting for that fragrance, but it is still there, still the same, intoxicating to us who know it, still redolent of all the years of happiness, and now someone else will breathe it, someone who doesn't know its meaning at all.

How shall we say goodbye to the glory of that house, how accept the sadness that it is no longer ours? By making it, as Schmemann says, of time, the object of our Christian faith and action. By recognizing that time has two dimensions—it brings things to an end, and it gives us always new beginnings. Christ is the Alpha and the Omega, the beginning and the end, and we bring to him all of our beginnings and endings, all the hope and sadness that they cause us, all of the work done and the pleasures enjoyed as well as all our plans for work to be done and pleasures to be enjoyed.

> *"So, through life, death, through sorrow, and*
> *through sinning,*
> *He shall suffice me, for He hath sufficed.*
> *Christ is the End, for Christ was the Beginning,*
> *Christ the Beginning, for the End is Christ.*
> —F.W.H. Meyer, "St. Paul"

We give thanks, then, as we bring these things to him, and in the giving of thanks we signal our total acceptance of his will for us.

* * *

We are also granted temporary reprieves. Aunt Clara called the other night to say that it's not going on the market after all. Not exactly, anyway. She has figured out some kind of plan which may make the place available to family members for a little while longer.

There is a storybook sort of attic in the Cottage, with two bedrooms built into it originally as servants' rooms. As our family expanded I slept in one of these instead of in the bedroom on the second floor with the bird's-eye maple and bamboo furniture. This room had an old-fashioned bed, bureau and wooden washstand on which stood a great brown-and-white china basin, a soapdish to match, and two pitchers, large and small. Inside the little door that opened at the bottom of the washstand was a matching chamberpot. The most interesting feature of this room, however, was what my aunt called her rogues' gallery, a long row of black-and-white photographs of her female college classmates, all with demure waves dipping low over the forehead, all with the peculiarly ill-fitting blouses of the thirties, all with the same bland and trustful expression, gazing mildly down at me as I lay in the bed. My aunt called them girls. To me they were most certainly not girls. They had been to college, they were old, they were unknown and unapproachable, and the unrelieved sameness of hairdo, expression and costume created in my mind a distant strange world of which I would never be a part.

Under the attic eaves were other things which had the same effect. There was a small trunk of the variety made to fit nicely on the top of a stagecoach. This had belonged to great-great Aunt Annie of (I knew from her photographs) rigid posture, black silk dresses and only the faintest hint of a smile. There were also woodcuts depicting Adam and Eve confronting Satan, or angels and cherubim and stallions and obese ladies in impossible positions. These had been relegated to the attic, probably by my mother, "because they gave the children nightmares," but I suspected it was because every one of them portrayed one or more beings, celes-

33

tial or terrestrial, who in her opinion were not adequately clothed. These my bothers and I crawled into the dusty recesses to study at our leisure. To this day Satan appears in my imagination with the same fierce and wicked face of those woodcuts, although I have managed to improve on the images of Adam and Eve.

The tiny brown field mice with delicate pink feet which ran up and down the electric wires and scattered seeds among the picture frames and mattresses of the attic were my friends. I would lie on my stomach holding my breath, not moving an eyelash, waiting for them to appear at their holes in the floorboards. I felt with them a special kinship in that we were the living denizens of this attic—intruders, perhaps, but here and alive, in spite of Satan and the cherubs, the great-great aunt and the college "girls" who were here long before we came.

There was a lovely pine grove behind the Cottage with a path that ran through it to what Aunt Annie had named "The Meeting of the Waters," junction of two clear mountain streams, Gale River and Pond Brook. Wooden seats had been constructed encircling several of the larger pine trees, and when I was very small my grandfather took me to sit on one of them while he showed me how to build a house of twigs on the floor of the forest.

My aunt taught me the wild flowers that grew near the Cottage, and I pressed them in a brown dime store notebook—cinquefoil, Quaker lady and twin flower from the pine woods, wild orchid and lady's slipper from the low, grassy place at the river's level, devil's paintbrush, butter-and-eggs, goldenrod and Queen Anne's lace from the meadow in front of the Cottage. Years later I learned the bracken, ferns and mosses, and showed other small children the wonders of the hairy cap moss—how you take off its hairy cap, lift the lid of the tiny "salt shaker," and pour out its pale green powder into the palm of your hand.

There were our fields, our own woods, our swimming place down at the Meeting of the Waters. The very rocks belonged, we felt, to us. In the field were three large granite rocks, too heavy to move when the rest were cleared for planting long before. My brothers and I each claimed one of these as our own. We would go out and "ride" them, imagining ourselves mounted on an elephant, a camel and a tortoise. There was "The Big Rock," a gigantic boulder in the middle of Gale River with a deep pool beside it to swim in. Occasionally there was a trout and often we caught the bigger fish we always called suckers. The rock had a beautiful flat top where you could toast yourself after coming out of the frigid water, feeling the warmth of the sun on one side of you and the warmth of the rock on the other.

All of this, then, was ours—even the intoxicating smell of the cold brooks running over the clean stones between the sun-warmed pine and spruce-covered banks. The land on the far side of Pond Brook belonged, in my mind, to God. It was wilderness. There were no trails but animal trails there, and we felt that there were deer and maybe now and then a bear.

We grew up in the Depression, and although we had no idea we were poor, we had little idea how rich we were in things other than money. That Cottage was one of the great riches, with its treasures inside and its priceless scenery outside, its inexhaustible supply of things to do, things to look at and smell and revel in, the mountains to climb and the woods to explore, the streams to bathe in, the rocks to own.

When I go back there now there is, mingled with the smell of spruce, the smell of char-broiled steaks floating across meadow and stream. There's a campground now in God's own wilderness. If ever the

35

deer and the bear were really there as we hoped, they are gone, replaced by campers, tents, trailers and displaced people on that inevitably fruitless quest for what isn't there. They don't listen to the wind in the trees or the brooks flowing over rocks. They've got the transistor radio on full volume while they set up the outdoor grill. They don't lie in the dark and look at the moon over Lafayette—they've just pumped up the pressure lantern or switched on the lights that have by this time, for all I know, been wired in across the brook. They wade into our stream and climb over the Big Rock and toss their beer cans down where the suckers used to be.

I have to get a firm grip on myself and remember that none of this deprives me of what I had. "All that was ever ours," wrote Amy Carmichael of India, "is ours forever." That wonderful place was one of the stations of my life. It helped to shape my tastes and loves and imagination and vision of God, and I remember his command to the people of Israel, "Thou shalt remember all the way which the Lord thy God led thee . . ."

They were to remember all of it. Most of it, I suppose, was more boring than memorable on that desert journey, and they had to go from Point A to Point B to Point C and all the way to Point Z in obedience, whether or not anything interesting happened along the way. But there were special places where God met them in special ways, and thus he helped them to review his leading. He knew how their memory would need jogging. The Cottage is one of the stations I go back to in my memory with joy. There are, of course, other kinds of places as well, places not at all like the Cottage which I would as soon forget. But, as Phillips Brooks prayed, I pray, "O Lord, by all Thy dealings with us, whether of light or darkness, of joy or pain, let us be brought to Thee." It is he to whom and with whom we travel, and while he is the End of our journey, he is also at every stopping-place.

Boredom

IN THE BOOK *A Sort of Life* Graham Greene tells how he has struggled, ever since he was very young, to fend off boredom. He once had a dentist extract ("but with ether") a perfectly good tooth for no better reason than that he was bored and this seemed like an interesting diversion. He tried several times to commit suicide and six times played Russian roulette, using a revolver with six chambers—a dangerous game, but not, heaven help us, boring.

Dorothy Parker was famous for her wit before she was 30. She had great charm, a fine education, a fascinating kind of beauty and many interesting friends. But she was utterly bored. She too thought of suicide, and was quoted in John Keats' book *You Might As Well Live* as saying:

> *Razors pain you;*
> *Rivers are damp;*
> *Acids stain you;*
> *And drugs cause cramp.*
> *Guns aren't lawful;*
> *Nooses give;*
> *Gas smells awful;*
> *You might as well live.*

Her life story seemed to me the exact illustration of acedia, or accidie, which is an old word for boredom, but a word that includes depression, sloth, irritability, lazy languor and bitterness. "This rotten sin," wrote Chaucer, "maketh a man heavy, wrathful and raw." Poor Miss Parker had been so irritable and raw with people—she had treated even her friends unspeakably badly—that she spent her last years alone in a hotel in New York, her pitiful, neglected dogs and her liquor bottles almost her only companions.

Gertrude Behanna says, on her record, "God Isn't Dead," that she has come to believe that it is a real sin to bore people. When we stop to think about it, most of us would readily agree. But how many of us have thought of boredom itself, so long as it affects only ourselves, as a sin? The Bible speaks of joy as a Christian virtue. It is one of the fruits of the Spirit, and often we find that it characterizes the people of God whose stories we read in the Bible. The worship of God in the Old Testament was accompanied by the most hilarious demonstrations of gladness—dancing, shouting and music-making. (This was to me one of the most impressive features of life in modern Israel when I visited there.)

Joy is not a word we use much nowadays. We think of it poetically as the opposite of sorrow, another word that does not often come into conversation. Both words represent experiences one does not normally have every day.

But I think we are mistaken. I think joy is meant to be an everyday experience, and as such it is the exact opposite of boredom, which seems to be the everyday experience (am I being overly pessimistic?) of most Americans. I get the impression that everybody is always hoping for a chance to get away from it all, relax, unwind, get out of these four walls, find somewhere, somehow, some action or excitement. Advertising, of course, has done a splendid job of creating in us greed for things we would never have thought of wanting, and thereby convincing us that whatever we have is

39

intolerably boring. Attributing human wants to animals, we easily swallow the TV commercials that tell us that Morris the cat doesn't want tunafish every day, he wants eight different flavors.

"Godliness with contentment is great gain." Those words were written a long time ago to a young man by an older man who had experienced almost the gamut of human suffering, including being chained day and night to a prison guard. Contentment is another word which has fallen into disuse. We think of it, perhaps, in connection with cows—the best milk comes from contented ones, doesn't it?—but it doesn't take much to content a cow. Peace and fodder are probably all it asks. We are not cows. What does it take to content us? How could Paul, after what he had been through, write as he did to Timothy?

C.S. Lewis, one of the most godly and civilized men I have ever heard of, exemplified what Paul was getting at. Lewis wrote that he was never bored by routine. In fact, he said, he liked it. He had what his anthologist Clyde S. Kilby called "a mind awake." Why should routine spoil it? Pictures of him show a joyful man. But he was not a man unacquainted with poverty, hard work and suffering any more than Paul was. He knew them, but he knew too what lay beyond. "All joy," he wrote to a friend, "(as distinct from mere pleasure, still more amusement) emphasizes our pilgrim status; always reminds, beckons, awakens desire. Our best havings are wantings."

Those wantings lie in the deepest places of our being, and they are for the kind of joy that, according to Lewis, is "the serious business of heaven." So we waste our time, our money and our energies when we pursue so frantically the pleasures which we hope will bring us relief from boredom. We end up bored with everything and everybody. Work which can be joyful if accepted as a part of the eternal order and a means to

40

serve, becomes only drudgery. Our pettiest difficulties, not to mention our big ones, are cause for nothing but complaint and self-pity. All circumstances not deliberately arranged by us look like obstacles to be rid of. We consume much and produce little, we get depressed and depression is actually dangerous and destructive.

But there is another way. Paul made it perfectly clear that his contentment had nothing to do with how desirable his circumstances were. "I am content with weaknesses, insults, hardships, persecutions and calamities." It is no list of amusements. How, then, did it work? It worked by a mysterious transforming power, something that reversed things like weakness and hardship, making them into strength and joy. Is there any chance that it will work for us? Is there for us, too, an antidote for boredom? The promise of Christ was not for Paul alone. "My grace is sufficient for you." It's a gift to be accepted. If we refuse it, nothing will be enough and boredom will be the story of our lives.

Truth Telling

I BUILT a house in New Hampshire a few years ago. The bulldozing for the foundation had barely begun when a shiny car drove up and out stepped a man dressed in very clean work clothes. He took off his hard hat and introduced himself as "the best gosh-darn well-driller in the whole North Country." I needed a well, and he drilled it and did a good job. After that he would drop by whenever he had work in the neighborhood. The coffee I gave him was a small price to pay to hear him talk. He held opinions about everything and was afraid of nothing and nobody. And he certainly knew how to tell a story. I listened enthralled. He had his own way of running a business ("We need your business—our business is going in the hole" was his motto, painted on the side of his drilling rigs) and his own code of ethics, both of which worked fine for him.

"I've worked for people, and I'm not lying to you," he said one day. "You can call my wife right up and she'll go over the checkbook, and I'll bet you over the last five years there's been fifteen people I've gone and drilled a well for and give 'em 2 percent off if they pay in ten days. Well, like the money'd be coming from the bank or something and it might go thirty days and the people were honest, they wouldn't take their 2 percent and I'd send it back. Now how many guys will send back money once they get it? Like, it'd be a two-thousand-dollar job and that'd be, what, twenty dollars? Yeah. You can ask my wife and she'll show you the checkbook. Because I just don't do things that way, I mean that, life's too short.

"Now let's say you're in business. You're doin' something so let's say I go and say, 'Well, heck, don't hire Betty Elliot, she don't know what she's doin'.' Well, all right, they may go and hire you anyway and you may do the best job in the world. Now isn't that gonna make me look stupid? Sometimes I go to look at a job and a guy'll say to me he can get somebody else to drill his well for six dollars a foot when I'm asking seven. I'll say to him, 'You know I didn't come up here to give you an education about my competition, I never give 'em a thought. All I know is I know what I'm doin' and I've got something to show for it. If you need this well drilled I can drill it. As far as I'm concerned half my competition stinks, but if you want to ask me to come here to see you about a well I'm not comin' here to run down my competition because the idea of it is you might hire one of my competitors and he might do a wonderful job and then you can say, 'Well, I don't know what on earth he was shootin' off his mouth about.' I can't see that kind of business, can you? Life's too short.

"But the way I look at life is that no matter who it is—so long as they're somewheres near square—everybody's gotta get a living. I mean I'm not planning to drill all the wells, but so what if I don't? I do what I can, and I do it good. The other guy's gotta eat, he's got a wife and kids, too, so what's the difference?

"I never charge anything for setting up the rig, either. A lot of guys, they want three hundred dollars for setting up and they want their money the day they're done drillin', but then if you got to put the pump in and there's something wrong, well, what're you gonna do? You've had it, and you've got to stop payment on a check, you gotta work fast. But I don't do things that way. I'm not interested in it. But you've gotta go out there and do something and life is short. If you gotta be crooked on everything you do and you can't look people in the face, you know full well they think you're a crook and it's a pretty short world to be doin' that all the time, I would say."

It is a short world, and it doesn't take more brains than most of us have to figure out that honesty is a good thing if it helps business and keeps us from looking too stupid. It's the best policy, obviously, but it isn't usually much more than that. It's one of those things, along with eating and dieting, taxation, religion and loving your neighbor, that we all feel can be carried too far. Too far, that is, if the matter concerns ourselves.

"The people in your organization are certainly the most honest bunch I've ever seen," a woman said to a friend of mine.

"Honest? How do you mean?"

"Well, honest about each other."

We can stand a lot of honesty that concerns other people, and we jump to the defense of protesters so long as they're protesting things for which we're not directly responsible. But we are marvelously uncritical and generous when it comes right down to the nitty-gritty of our private lives. You won't catch us carrying things to extremes there.

People do overeat, but it hasn't been my problem. Dieting, on the other hand, can be carried too far and that piece of pie does look delicious. As for religion, a good thing, of course—an excellent thing if you don't get too much of it at once. And I'm willing to pay my taxes. I understand that the country can't run without them, but this bill, now. . . . Loving my neighbor? I do. But how far do you think a person ought to be expected to go anyhow?

At a camp where my husband worked for several summers the counselors had to grade each camper on certain character traits. Was he, for example, exceptionally, moderately or fairly honest?

Last year a man in Elmhurst, Illinois, found two Brinks money bags containing $183,000. He threw them, unopened, into the trunk of his car and for four days wondered what to do with them. (He mentioned later that he did not even think to tell his wife. I think she would have known what to do.)

"I didn't know it was money," he told newsmen. "I thought it might be mail. I forgot about them until I began reading stories in the paper. Then I realized what I had. I had always daydreamed about finding a lot of money, but it became a reality and things changed. I had to call."

Asked why he didn't break the seals on the bags he said, "You don't break seals on people's parcels. That would muddle things considerably. I'm an honest man within reasonable limits."

The Brinks company awarded him $18,000 for his honesty, which raises the question of whether his was, in fact, a "reasonable" honesty, for if he had been dishonest he might possibly have succeeded in keeping the $183,000 for himself, along with, at the very least, some sleepless nights.

It is a short world, and if this is the only world, we can play it like a game—fair and somewheres near square. That ought to be good enough, and a man ought to be allowed to get what he's willing to pay for.

But what about gaining the whole world and losing your own soul? Those words apply to another world altogether, the long one, where the rules are not the same at all, where things like poverty and meekness and sorrow and hunger and purity of heart lead to happiness. Then, too, the Rule Book has things about living "honestly in all things," "providing for honest things, not only in the sight of the Lord, but also in the

45

sight of men," and (who can stand up to this one?) about the Lord's desiring "truth in the inward parts." It is what I would have to call an unreasonable honesty, beyond any of us, and we have to call out, "Lord, save me!" And that is what he does.

And recently I met a friend for lunch whom I had not seen for twenty years. As I approached the restaurant I was thinking the usual thoughts: Will she have changed much? Will I recognize her? Will we be able to find things to talk about?

I saw her as soon as I got there, and I knew that if I said, "Why, Helen, you haven't changed a bit!" it would be a bald lie. The truth was that Helen was beautiful now. She had never been a beauty in college. The years and her experiences (some of them of a kind of suffering I knew nothing about) had given her a deep womanliness, a kind of tender strength. Her eyes glowed, there was passion about her mouth, and the lines of her face revealed a strength of character she could not have had when she was a college student. So, instead of the usual pleasantries, I simply started with the truth. I told her what I saw in her face. Of course she was taken aback, but I am sure that this unorthodox beginning did not render further conversation more difficult. We were able to get down to the real things in life, things that matter and that had changed us both, rather than spending an hour on the ages of our children, their mates and careers, our latest diets and recipes.

We all know that the truth often hurts. We use this cliché as a defense for having hurt someone, and sometimes it is indeed necessary to tell this kind of truth. But there is truth which does not hurt—truth which encourages and surprises with delight and gratitude. What if a teacher sees that a colleague of hers has succeeded in breaking down the resistance of a pupil who has been the despair of the other teachers, the talk of the faculty lunch room? The change in the student is noticed, a sigh of relief is heaved, but who goes to the teacher herself and says, "Thanks! You've done what the rest of us couldn't do!" How many are free enough from themselves to recognize the worth of others and to speak of it honestly?

A lady who is a good many years older than I tells me often of the aunt who was a mother to her throughout her childhood. "Auntie" impressed her with the need to tell the truth—the welcome kind—and she would add emphatically, "Tell them now." My friend calls me on the telephone—sometimes to thank me for a note or a little gift, sometimes to tell me what my friendship means to her.

"You remember what Auntie always said," she will say, "So, I'm telling you now." There would be no way for me to exaggerate how she has cheered and helped me.

I was talking with a lady who had been a missionary for forty years, and I noticed that she had exceptionally lovely hands. "Has anyone ever told you your hands are beautiful?" I asked. The dear soul was so flustered one might have thought I had committed an indecency. She looked at her hands in amazement.

"Why . . . why no. I don't think anyone ever has!" But she saw that I meant it, and she had the grace to hear the truth. She said thank you.

Tell it like it is is the watchword today. But suppose it's lovely? Suppose it's actually beautiful? C. S. Lewis said that the most fatal of all nonconductors is embarrassment. It seems to me that life is all too short to let embarrassment deprive us and our friends of the pleasure of telling the happy truth. Suppose the boy who does your lawn does it fast, trims it perfectly, and takes care of the tools? Suppose the clerk who waits on you happens to be the most gracious one you've ever encountered? Suppose even that your husband—when you stop for once to look at him, to think about him as a person and as a man—seems to you to be the best man you know?

Tell them.

Tell them now.

'M' Is for a Merry Heart

SPECIAL OCCASIONS like Mother's Day put different kinds of burdens on different people. Those whose work involves expressing themselves publicly usually feel that on such occasions they "ought to say something" appropriate to the day. At first I shied away from this, because I always shy away from things that might turn out to be soupy. But as I thought more about it I realized that it wasn't a question of "ought to" but a good excuse to write down just one or two things, at least, about a remarkable mother I know very well—my own. And if I write about her it won't be soupy.

She is nearly 72 years old now, and that fact, coupled with people's applying to her adjectives like "alert" and "spry" and "very much alive," reminds me that she is in the category of "old." People certainly don't use those adjectives much for other age groups. But it is hard to think of Katherine Gillingham Howard as old.

She lives alone in a house in Florida between some orange groves and a golf course. She makes good use of the groves but she hardly has time even to look at the golf course, let alone play on it. Time does not hang heavy on her hands, and one of the things she does with it is to keep up a steady and cheerful correspondence with her six married children and her fifteen grandchildren. We write to her, make carbons of our letters, and she writes to all of us and sends the carbons around every week.

She has taken a lot of teasing in her life with us, and we still tease her in letters and she teases back. She is one of those people who knows how to laugh, hard. When you stop to think of it, how many people in your acquaintance can laugh hilariously, until tears roll down their faces?

And one of the things we never let her alone about is the way she uses emotionally loaded words. Three of the six of us grew up during the Depression and were taught many small economies, including turning off lights and things. If Mother found a light left on where it wasn't needed, the light was blazing. A radio in an empty room was not just on, it was blaring. A child with no clothes on was not merely naked, he was running around naked. (Of course I'm not saying my mother is the only one who does this. People have asked me I don't know how many times, of the Indian tribe I knew in Ecuador, "Do you mean to say they just run around completely naked?" The idea of people doing quite ordinary things like sitting still or cooking with no clothes on seems to be a hard one to grasp.)

It was not possible, apparently, for Mother simply to take the children downtown. Children were dragged downtown and through the stores. If our friends came to visit us after school they traipsed through the kitchen, traipsed upstairs, traipsed through the bedrooms.

No matter how poor we were my parents somehow contrived to have a guest room and it was frequently filled. Mother was a good hostess, and it seemed we were always meeting trains in Philadelphia or boats in New York that had missionaries on them, and we understood that it was a privilege to have guests in our home. Schoolboys who came home with my brothers on holidays from boarding school were in a separate category in my mother's mind, I think, though she was very sweet about having them. They were always clattering

50

up and down stairs, sloshing around in the bathroom and bumping down the halls with suitcases.

My father—very tall, very studious and very fond of the outdoors—was not much good at all around the house, but occasionally he would try to spare Mother some work by fixing his own or, on very rare occasions, her breakfast. It never turned out especially well because she lay in bed, stark staring awake, and had to listen to him rattling around in the kitchen.

Mother's cooking was strictly sensible, plain and nourishing, and she was an expert at meat and potatoes. (She was raised, my father used to say, on roast beef, while he was brought up on fried smelts, Beauregard eggs and jelly.) She had no time for fancy salads or dessert. Fresh or canned fruit and store-bought cookies were a fairly standard dessert because they didn't require fiddling.

When I came home from boarding school I felt that the menus at home were just too, too ordinary. "Well," said Mother, not much moved, "you just go ahead and do all the fiddling you want."

If she was talking about a shopping trip to Germantown, which she loved (she had grown up there and no one could ever convince her that there were stores elsewhere equal to Germantown's), she said she would "just run over there." If she was talking about one of my father's numerous speaking engagements, which were sometimes burdensome, he wouldn't run over, he would have to trail way out to Fox Chase or Doylestown.

A single woman named Daphne, who was always on the edge of financial ruin and therefore had to make do with a succession of battered old cars, never just drove to see us, she came trundling down the turnpike.

Well, it must have been quite a life for her. You wonder how anybody survives all the blazing lights, blaring radios, dragging of children, traipsing, clattering, sloshing and bumping, rattling around, fiddling, trailing and trundling. Now that we have children of our own we know what she means, and increasingly appreciate the color and jollity of the life she made for us. We know, too, that there was a far deeper source of strength than her "merry heart" which, as the writer of the Proverbs said, "doeth good like a medicine." She often needed a great deal more than merriment—she needed a Rock that was higher than she. She found him, and with my father, she led us to him. We are grateful for that, and for what she put up with, and if you were to ask her now to tell about it, it would not sound chaotic or pitiable at all, I think. She would admit that she used all those vivid words, all right, but she would never have thought of them as loaded, and she would probably have to wipe her eyes for laughing at the pictures they recall.

The Shock of Self-Recognition

MOST OF US are rather pleased when we catch sight of ourselves (provided the sight is sufficiently dim or distant) in the reflection of a store window. It is always amusing to watch people's expressions and postures change, perhaps ever so slightly, for the better as they look at their images. We all want the reflected image to match the image we hold in our minds (e.g. a rugged, casual slouch goes well with a Marlboro country type; an erect distinguished carriage befits a man of command and responsibility). We glimpse ourselves in a moment of lapse, and quickly try to correct the discrepancies.

A close-up is something else altogether. Sometimes it's more than we can stand. The shock of recognition makes us recoil. "Don't tell me that's my voice!" (on the tape recorder); "Do I really look that old?" (as this photograph cruelly shows). For me it is a horrifyingly painful experience to have to stand before a three-way mirror, in strong light, in a department-store fitting room. ("These lights—these mirrors—they distort, surely!" I tell myself.) I have seen Latin American Indians whoop with laughter upon first seeing themselves on a movie screen, but I have never seen them indignant, as "civilized" people often seem to be. Perhaps it is that an Indian has not occupied himself very much with trying to be what he is not.

What is it that makes us preen, recoil, laugh? It must

53

be the degree of incongruity between what we thought we were and what we actually saw.

People's standards, of course, differ. Usually, in things that do not matter, we set them impossibly high and thus guarantee for ourselves a life of discontent. In things that matter we set them too low and are easily pleased with ourselves. (My daughter came home from the seventh grade one day elated. "Missed the honor roll by two C's!" she cried, waving her report card happily.) Frequently we judge by standards that are irrelevant to the thing in question. You have to know what a thing is for, first of all, before you can judge it at all. Take a can opener—how can I know whether it's any good unless I know that it was made for opening cans?

Or a church. What is it for? Recently the one I belong to held a series of neighborhood coffee meetings for the purpose of finding out what the parishioners thought about what the church was doing, was not doing and ought to be doing. The results were mailed to us last week. Eighty people participated and came up with one hundred and five "concerns and recommendations." These revealed considerable confusion as to what the church is meant to be about. "Should have hockey and basketball teams." "There is too much reference to the Bible in sermons." "The ushers should stop hunching at the doors of the church and seek out unfamiliar faces." "The rear parking lot is messy." "A reexamination of spiritual goals should be carried out." I was glad there were a few like that last one. The range of our congregational sins was pretty well covered (we didn't get into the mire of our personal ones), and as I read them over I thought, "If we just managed to straighten out these one hundred and five things we'd have—what? Well, something, I suppose. But not a perfect church. Not by a long shot. If by our poor standards (some of them obviously applicable to

54

things other than churches) we picked out over a hundred flaws, how many were visible to God, 'to whose all-searching sight the darkness shineth as the light?"

There are times when it is with a kind of relief that we come upon the truth. A man passing a church one day paused to see if he could catch what it was the people were mumbling in unison. He moved inside and heard the words: "We have erred and strayed from thy ways like lost sheep. We have followed too much the devices and desires of our own hearts. We have offended against thy holy laws."

"Hmm," thought the man, "they sound like my kind of people."

"We have left undone those things which we ought to have done, and we have done those things which we ought not to have done."

"This is the church for me," he decided. (I don't suppose a basketball team or a black-topped parking lot would have persuaded him.)

"Put up a complaint box and you'll get complaints," my husband used to say. There is something to be said for airing one's grievances, and there is a great deal to be said for not airing them, but one thing at least seems good to me—that we be overwhelmed, now and then, with our sins and failures.

We need to sit down and take stock. We need mirrors and neighborhood coffees and complaint boxes, but our first reaction may be despair. Our second, "Just who does so-and-so think he is, criticizing the church when he never even comes to church?" And we find ourselves back where we started, setting our own standards, judging irrelevantly and falsely, excusing ourselves, condemning an institution for not being what it was never meant to be, and so on.

The church, thank God, has provided for us. There is Lent. It is a time to stop and remember. All year we have had the chance in the regular communion service to remember the death and passion of the Lord Jesus, and this once during the year we are asked, for a period of six weeks, to recall ourselves, to repent, to submit to special disciplines in order that we may understand the meaning of the Resurrection.

We are indeed "miserable offenders." We have done and left undone. We are foolish and weak and blind and self-willed and men of little faith. We run here, we run there, we form committees and attend meetings and attack the church and its organization and its isolation and its useless machinery and its irrelevance and ineffectiveness. But all the time it stands there, holding the Cross, telling us that there is forgiveness, that we have not been left to ourselves, that no matter how shocking the image that we finally see of ourselves in the light of God's truth, God himself has done something about it all.

"He was wounded for our transgressions. He was bruised for our iniquities." For the very things we've been discussing. For the things that make us moan and groan and ask, "What's the use?"

And so Lent, simply because it is another reminder of him who calls us to forgiveness and refreshment, makes me glad.

Mind the Gap

I HAVE BEEN to London only once in my life and I was, to use a word I don't toss around carelessly, thrilled by it. There was ruggedness, dignity, massiveness and strength there that entered into my soul. There was also, I thought, laughter at the heart of it. The English, for all their reputation of stolidity and sobriety, give out a kind of humor that I love—sort of offhand, half repressed. I found myself laughing with and at them and also at myself as a visiting American. In the London subways (so amazingly clean, fast and deep underground) a voice comes over the public address system as a train pulls into the station. In full, round Cockney the voice booms, "Mind the gap!" Signs over the tracks repeat the message. I was bewildered by it until I saw that the platform is so shaped that there is a gap between it and some sections of the train. "Mind the gap" is a clear, short way of warning you to notice that there is one, and to be careful how you cross it.

It doesn't take any special perspicacity to notice nowadays that there is another sort of gap. You know the one I mean—the generation gap. I mind it, but only in the English sense. I know it's there, I try to be careful how I cross it. But I don't mind it at all in the American sense. I like it.

Robert Frost wrote, "Something there is that does not love a wall." I go along with that—there is something, but it's not me. All my life I have loved the New

England stone walls undulating through the hilly pastures and along the roads. I learned to love the four plain walls of a house when I had to live for a number of months without any. "A wall," wrote Leopold Tyrmand in *The New Yorker* a few months ago, "in spite of its frequent misuse, remains one of civilization's basic inventions; we have as much need of being separated as of being together." Some primitive peoples, including the Indians with whom I was living, like togetherness enough to live without walls. Some presumably civilized peoples are getting to like it more and more, but it seems to me an uncivilized idea. Togetherness is all very well in certain very limited circumstances—in a family, for instance, up to a point. But even there it won't work unless there is God-given love.

The love that comes from God is the only kind that properly minds the gaps. His love appreciates distinctions, respects privacy and recognizes the variety which he has put into his marvelous world, variety which makes for excitement and fun. Who doesn't like to watch people, to study the differences in faces, behavior, dress and speech? Isn't variety a part of the joy of collecting things like shells or rocks, or of studying astronomy, botany, ornithology?

Only yesterday a friend told me her teen-age daughter's response to a certain minister who had grown sideburns and learned "rock" language in order to "turn on the teen-agers."

"He turns me right off!" the girl said. "Boy, if there's anything that turns me off, it's an adult trying to act like a teen-ager. Who's he kidding?"

I had heard this man speak and had come away with the impression that, in his opinion, few of us older ones have any idea "where it's at." We're not "communicating." I agree that communication, anywhere, anytime, may present difficulties, and we are often guilty of creating gaps which ought not to exist, or closing gaps which ought to, instead of learning how best to bridge those that do. But I could not escape the feeling that this man somehow hoped that his wide necktie and bell-bottom trousers would prove to younger people that he was with it. He hoped to be able to talk to them because he'd taken on some of their fads. Perhaps he succeeded, but I protest that his method is not for all.

I know a man, more than twice the "trustworthy" age, who, if it is too much to claim that he "turns kids on," at least reaches them. He does not wear sideburns, he does not wear bell-bottoms, he hates guitar music, he takes showers every day, he is a college professor and a square. But for some reason his students listen to him. They keep signing up for his courses, like him and come to him. They see in him, I am convinced, a real man. They recognize a man who believes something, lives by it, knows how to get it across to them. They know that there's a gap, and a wide one, between him and them. Therefore they have something to "mind," something to think about, to strive toward.

On several occasions when I have been invited to speak to student groups, I have asked this question: "Is there any adult in your life whom you truly admire?" Seldom is there an immediate response. They have to stop and think of at least one who has influenced them for good and won their admiration.

My next question is: "What is it about that person that made an impact?" These answers (also slow in coming) generally illustrate the importance of gaps. These were people set apart from the rest in some way. All of them, I find, were considered real people—a man was a real man, a woman was a real woman. Perhaps the person was also a foreigner or a cripple or very old or in some other obvious way different from the general run of people. But this difference, far from turning the student on, appears in some cases to have been a factor in the degree of influence.

The admired was, in all cases, something the admirer was not. There was a gap. It was noticeable and was accepted. These people accepted themselves for what they were, as well as accepting the responsibility that came with being who they were, and they stood on their convictions.

They also bridged the gap somehow. They had, in one way or another, reached out to that student from where they were, recognized him and moved over whatever divisions were between them in a way which made them welcome.

We hate intrusion. This is why we need walls. But we hate isolation also. The young howl because there is a generation gap. "Why don't the old understand us? Why don't they accept us for what we are?" But then the young want to be left alone. They want their own thing and sometimes even expect the old to like it. The old in turn howl because the gap is there. "Why can't the young be like us? Why all this foolishness and rejection of our values?"

Let us back off a little. Aren't certain differences meant to be there? Isn't there something to be said for preservation of distinctions?

Mind the gaps—between men and women (God help us all if the idea of Unisex gets hold of us), between the stage and audience in a theater (I don't want an actor coming up my aisle), between those who know and those who don't know (let teachers teach, please, don't make them forever ask, What do you think?), and between the generations (let the young be young with all their hearts, and let me be old and admit it gracefully).

And let me—let all of us—be humble enough to be enriched by what someone else is that I am not.

Housework and High-flown Ideas

I HAD MADE up my mind several weeks ago that I would probably have to write something sometime about women's liberation. I wouldn't be able to endure it in silence much longer. Before I came downstairs to write (I have a nice little study in my basement), I washed the breakfast dishes, made a bed, took my husband to work, wrapped up a birthday package for a nephew and fixed some marinade for the Rock Cornish hens we're having for dinner tonight. All fairly routine tasks, but I loved every minute. Loved every minute? Yes, that's what I said, and that's what I mean by getting off to a bad start. Strident female voices keep telling us publicly that it's time we women threw off the shackles of domestic labor because it's not self-fulfilling. That term gags me, but more of that later.

This morning I found myself dawdling over the dishes. It wasn't because I hate them but because I like them, and I was not overly anxious to be liberated from the job so that I could come down to the typewriter and do something "creative" (another word that is beginning to gag me). I caught myself softly singing a song (I don't usually sing when I'm alone, but sometimes I whisper songs) as I looked out at the New England autumn, my hands in hot water, my feet on a firm, clean floor. I am not at all that used to having nice china, a car to drive, a carpet to vacuum and a choice of menus for dinner, let alone someone to do all this for. I happen to be one of those (and the world is full of them) who went without such things for a good share of my adult life, and I haven't yet got over being grateful.

I saw a woman on TV the other day who looked more like a picturebook witch than anybody I've ever seen. I wondered at first what children's program I had stumbled on. Then I heard her name—one that's too often in the headlines these days—and she was giving it to us hammer and tongs. Stop being unpaid housekeepers! I stopped in my tracks. Unpaid housekeepers? Oh, come on now, I said to her. What sort of pay do you want, anyway? It depends, I suppose, on what sort of woman you are. I, for one, will keep house for love, but not for money. Not on your life. And who said anybody had to keep house? As I recall, my husband asked me to marry him. He made a proposal. I liked it, so I took it. It was purely voluntary, and I had no trouble volunteering.

Women are badly mixed up about this equality thing. What on earth do they mean? "If we mean that all are equally useful or beautiful or good or entertaining," wrote that sensible man C.S. Lewis—and he was speaking of mankind in general—"then it is nonsense."

Almost all of the avalanche of words we read and hear from the female "liberators" is idle talk. I can go along with the idea of equality in political and economic areas. Of course women should vote. Of course they should be paid what men are paid, if they do the same work. But in what other possible sense can any woman—any real woman, any sane woman, I mean—wish equality? Is there no order to be recognized in the universe itself; no hierarchy, no harmony of differences?

I have mentioned before my particular liking for gaps—for example, the one the French appreciate between the sexes *(Vive la difference!)*. Stamp out discrimination! scream the feminists. Take it slowly, I plead. Make sure you know what sort of discrimination you're talking about before you hoist the banner. I, for one, know a man when I see one. I would like to be sure I can still tell a woman from a man. One of those captivating Gabor sisters (I can't remember which is which, but they are unmistakably women) told David Frost, in answer to his questions about women's liberation, that she thinks they are all crazy. She has no complaints about being a woman.

A friend said to me wistfully one day, concerning the dishpan and the typewriter, "But you can find self-fulfillment in your writing." Hmm. What shall I say to someone who thinks that? I have thought over the idea in my solitary hours. Self-fulfillment? Is that what I've found? Perhaps I should show her some of the letters I get. No, I won't do that. But if anyone says such a thing again I am going to try to tell her something like this:

First of all, I had no idea of self-fulfillment when I began to write. I got into it willy-nilly (a long story I'm not going to start on here). And I doubt very much if anything one gets himself into for the sake of self-fulfillment is likely to lead to anything but a sinkhole of—what else—selfishness.

The second thing is that writing, for me, is a painful business. There is a surprising number of people who entertain the secret conviction that only a lack of time and a good place to work prevent them from becoming best-selling authors. They may be right, and if they are, it is bad for my self-image, since I have both the time and the hideaway in the basement and I have never turned out a best seller. An awful lot of the time I spend trying to get things down on paper is a total loss, and an awful lot of what I get on paper goes eventually into the wastebasket. And I hate to think how much of what doesn't go there should have.

Housework is not like that. You don't start out with any foolish and high-flown ideas about creativity and all that. You can do it without concentrating, and you can count on the results. The dishes sparkle, the bed is smooth, the meal—even if the cake falls—gets eaten. Just because we have to do these things every day is not reason enough, in my opinion, for the whole world to be reminded unceasingly that the American housewife's state is a sad plight indeed.

"Ah, for a taste of the heady sweetness of independence!" sigh the unpaid drudges. I doubt that the sigh was ever sighed by many happily married women, or any widows. The latter group have had more than they want of that heady sweetness and have loathed becoming another strong-minded female. But a bit of strong-mindedness is necessary if a woman is to keep going by herself. She finds small sweetness in knowing that she has managed this or that alone.

Not me. I am afraid that I am just not women's lib material. I cannot be depended upon to take my happiness at the quotation of the day. I refuse to shoulder any chips of someone else's choice, to be told what I am to like and not to like. If I am suspect because I happen to think housework might turn out to be as fulfilling or creative as writing, if I must be carefully watched because the chores of a mother strike me as being at least as much fun as (no, I'll admit it, more than) those of a public speaker, I apologize. But not very sincerely.

C.S. Lewis says this, too:

"Equality is a quantitative term and therefore love often knows nothing of it. Authority exercised with humility and obedience accepted with delight are the very lines along which our spirits live."

There's the word—the one the women's liberationists

seem to have forgotten all about—love. And it's the word that ruins almost any good argument.

Recently I learned that one of the more sensible and clear-eyed Presbyterian ministers of my acquaintance is "swinging over to the 'woman-elder' side because of the weirdos pushing against ordination." Reasoning like that makes me want to shriek, rend my garments and throw dust into the air. I would be sorry in any case to learn that this particular minister favors the ordination of women—he was one of the few left that I was counting on to swim against the tide—but if he favors it in order not to have to keep company with weirdos he's probably jumping out of the frying pan into the fire. Which side has more weirdos?

I must confess I had no idea how weird I was myself until I read a book which has been enthusiastically welcomed among Christians, Nancy Hardesty and Letha Scanzoni's *All We're Meant to Be*. They answer some questions I had been too obtuse to ask, such as why God did not choose to send a female Messiah (she would have had little scriptural knowledge, for one thing, she would not have been permitted to teach in the synagogue or been listened to if she had, and—steady now—"with her monthly uncleanness making her ritually impure one fourth of the time, a female Messiah would have taken an extra year to complete God's mission"), how the word "head" carries no connotation of authority, and why we ought not to limit our references to God Almighty as *he*—for does not God refer to himself (there I go—my sexism is showing—why didn't I write "herself"?) as like a woman in travail, a mother, a hen, a woman sweeping her house? The authors suggest, in fact, that the pronoun "Thou" ought perhaps to be substituted for he/she, but their proposal does not include an explanation of how we are to do away altogether with the third

65

person singular and make do somehow only with the familiar second person when we speak of God. Are we to speak only to and never of him?

Another question was where in the world everybody has got the notion that the sexes have different functions? Nonsense, we are told. There's no such thing as separate spheres or different functions. All the myths, all the poetry, all the history of the world have led us down the garden path and it certainly isn't the Garden of Eden. Let's get back to reality and common sense and stop thinking of men as different from women, they say.

My head reels when I read all this, and I try to get my balance again. Ah, here is something solid. A passage of Scripture, from Ephesians 5: "You wives must learn to *adapt* yourselves to your husbands, as you *submit* yourselves in the Lord, for the husband is the *head* of the wife in the same way that Christ is *head* of the Church and savior of his body. The willing *subjection* of the Church to Christ should be reproduced in the *submission* of wives to their husbands. But, remember, this means that the husband must give his wife the same sort of love that Christ gave to the Church, when he sacrificed himself for her (italics mine)."

It sounds perfectly clear and understandable to me, and I have always thought I knew what it meant. "Adapt," "submit," "head"—simple words. And as with many other passages in the Bible, my problems have not been because I didn't understand it but because I understood it only too well. It's doing it that's hard. But no. Hardesty/Scanzoni tell us, referring to the above passage, "Don't get sidetracked by the words 'head' and 'subject' and their usual connotations." Sidetracked? When the word "head" occurs twice and the idea of submission occurs four times in a few short sentences? I begin to doubt whether I know how to read English at all. The authors, it seems to me, get

66

"sidetracked" by the idea of the husband's sacrificing himself for the wife—where did they come up with that idea if not from the self-same passage? Does the idea of sacrifice, which is certainly there, eclipse the idea of submission? They manage to expatiate on the passage for seven or eight pages without bothering to elucidate on what Paul meant by adaptation or subjection.

But then a long and impressive list of contrasts is drawn up between what is called the "traditional" view of women and a "new" or "another" ideology, and it was here that I learned the most startling things about myself. According to the categories established by the authors of *All We're Meant to Be,* I have been a lot of things I was never meant to be, and not half of the things I was meant to be, and it's all because I took a "traditional" view. I believed in a wife's obeying her husband and in a clear distinction between sexual roles and functions. Oddly enough, in such a state I have been quite content. But I am sure it is hoped that my "consciousness" will have been "raised," and I think it has. I found out, for example, that as a traditionalist I am also a sexist, whatever that means. Nobody has told me exactly, but it is a very bad word which seems to imply that I insist on recognizing and perpetuating *la difference.*

I, this book tells me, have been forced into playing a role—conforming to a stereotype. I never realized before that it was society, it was a "sinful" culture, it was a bunch of male chauvinists, who decided that the one who has the baby feeds it and changes its diapers. When my baby was born, I happened to be living in a culture entirely different from an American or European one, but the women in that culture had the same weird idea I had about what women were supposed to do. Of course, I was breaking rules, too, that I didn't know about. I was managing a crew of thirty or forty workmen, I was learning an unwritten language and trying to translate the Bible into it. I was handling the money in our family (at my husband's request) and generally mixing things up, it seems—for according to the authors' categories, it is only in the "new" ideology that a woman is permitted to manage, to think, to be "creative," "flexible," "imaginative," to have "maximum freedom to explore talents and interests." I was supposed to be "cramped," "restrained," and to feel like a "crushed automaton" with no identity. Alas! I did poorly at feeling that way.

I've had two marriages, both of them very short and very happy. Both of my husbands loved me, gave themselves to and for me, and to both of them I willingly and gladly submitted. But that was all a mistake, too, I have learned. Traditionally, I was supposed to be gritting my teeth and giving in grudgingly. A hierarchy is really nothing more than a tyranny; submission amounts to servility, self-destruction, the stifling of gifts, personhood, ability and spirit. A home where the husband is the head is the man's castle, all right, they tell me, but his wife is the janitor. Oh? I did poorly on that one, too. Even though the first five months of my married life were spent in a leaky tent in the jungle, I thought I was having a good time letting my husband go out and work on the airstrip with the Indians or preach to the little group gathered on Sundays, while I scrubbed clothes on an old-fashioned washboard, cooked on a tiny wood stove (mostly with wet wood), washed dishes in a basin with water hauled up a steep bank from a river. There's nothing "alive," "exciting," or "free" in that kind of life, now, is there— come now—was I anything more than a janitor? How long did I kid myself? Alas again!

Funny how all my married life I believed that the road to greatest happiness and fulfillment was self-giving love. As I understood the Bible, love for God

68

could best be expressed by submission and obedience to him, by denying myself, taking up my cross and following. I understood too that it was my privilege and my glad duty as a woman to adapt myself and submit to my husband in recognition of our respective assignments by a loving Creator-God. Whatever made me think that? Miss Hardesty and Mrs. Scanzoni inform me that nobody's in charge of a marriage except God. There's no other "head," the apostle Paul notwithstanding. It's a partnership, both parties exactly equal, accountable only to God, and that as a relationship or "companionship" or "covenant" neither can possibly have any authority over the other. (I thought that in my "relationship" or "companionship" or "covenant" with God he had authority. Are the ideas mutually exclusive?) Marriage was never a fifty-fifty proposition for me. I didn't want it to be because I understood that woman was made for man, but now it is claimed that nobody was made for anybody but God.

The "traditional" view of marriage, it is alleged, is characterized by fear and reluctant submission while by sharp contrast the "new" is characterized by love. This gives me an identity crisis. I don't know where I belong anymore. I had the impression during the few years I was a wife that I was living in love, that the whole thing was an "adventure of growth," a "continuous exchange," an "experience of self-actualization," a "direct participation in the world," and that we as a couple were "on the move." But I was way off. Only the "new" marriage, the "equal partnership," works that way. Whether I was aware of it or not, my "traditional" husbands required me to be immature; they built up their egos at my expense, allowed me no opinions of my own, kept me as a "docile childwife," made of me a weak, spiritless, dull, colorless, meek, subservient, passive creature. In short, our kind of marriage amounted to a "suicide of personality" for me.

Strange that I have no wish to do it over again the Hardesty-Scanzoni way. Strange that my memories of marriage are such happy ones and that I want to live out the rest of my life as a woman, even a single one, without the chips on my shoulder that certain feminists are trying to persuade me to carry.

In a Hospital Waiting Room

I HAVE been a patient in a hospital only once, when I was six years old and had my tonsils out. But during my husband's last illness I saw what that life was like. If you are in terrible pain or have broken an arm or a leg, the huge gray cluster of buildings can look like heaven, for inside are people who can do wonderful things to help. For a woman about to have a baby the hospital is full of anticipation of happiness. But for those who do not know what their disease may be, or who have been told that it is, finally, just what they most dreaded, the experience of going to the hospital can be an overpowering one of terror and horror and helplessness.

If one arrives in such a state, who can describe the effect of walking through the big glass doors into the bustling lobby of a city hospital where some rush around with many things to do and some wait? Nurses, doctors, visitors and ambulance drivers come and go. Others sit silently, some in wheelchairs (the ever-patient patients), waiting for someone, waiting to be taken somewhere, waiting for some dreaded or hoped-for word.

As we came through the doors a young man came toward us, using a new pair of crutches with the one leg left to him. A middle-aged couple wheeled a grown-up retarded son toward a waiting taxi. A stretcher with a blanketed form on it was brought in from a police ambulance. A very tall black youth carried two potted plants done up in rustling green paper.

People stood at the reception desk waiting to ask where to find a patient or a department or a doctor. The harried receptionist hardly looked at the questioners, giving out her short, practiced replies as though she had been affronted. We joined the line, got directions for the radiation department, and took the elevator to the fifth floor where we were told to follow the blue painted line on the hall floor. A boy who looked too young to be an orderly was pushing a wheelchair down the hall. A gray-haired lady sat in the chair weeping. Another boy raced around the corner, clipped the young orderly on the shoulder and the two exchanged some unintelligible banter behind the weeping woman's back.

We found the waiting room for the radiation department. It was nearly full, but we hung up our coats and found places to sit. I was in that state of exquisite sensitivity described so well in the Psalms in words such as these: "I am poured out like water, and all my bones are out of joint; my heart is like wax, it is melted within my breast; my strength is dried up like a potsherd, and my tongue cleaves to my jaws; thou dost lay me in the dust of the earth." Water, wax, broken pots, dust. Not much to fortify us there. "Lord, have mercy on us," I said (not aloud), "Christ, have mercy on us."

It was a winter afternoon and grew dark early. The only window in the room looked out on a gray brick wall.

A man with a large swelling on his neck, outlined in red ink, came in and put on his coat and left, his treatment over for that day. Then a little boy arrived with his mother. He had a red square with an X in it painted on each temple. Christ, have mercy on us. How can we endure?

72

The mother and son took off their coats, the mother sat down, but the boy was rambunctious and found things to do—messing up magazines, tipping over an ash tray, blowing out the match as his mother tried to light a cigarette.

Husbands and wives sat talking quietly and, I noticed, always kindly. One couple caught my attention particularly. They were shabbily dressed, and the man was badly crippled. It was the wife, however, who was there for radiation. I watched them talk to each other. They had courage, and they were quite evidently in love. Those who had been there before had become a fellowship. They waved, smiled, greeted each other. How could they? How did they manage to carry on in so normal a fashion?

Almost imperceptibly the picture began to take on a new color for me. An older lady in a pale green uniform came into the room, smiled at all of us, and asked if anyone would like coffee or ginger ale. I will always remember what that smile did for me, and the gracious, simple way in which she handed the beverages.

The nurse who came to call the patients for their treatments had a smile, too, and a cheerful voice (but not the forced cheerfulness of which nurses are so often accused). As she walked out of the waiting room with a patient, she put her arm around him. That touch (I wonder if she will ever know this?) was redemptive.

We had a long wait and I tried to read, but I kept looking up and watching what was going on in that crowded little room. The lady with the coffee I saw as our hostess, and I thought of the word "graciousness," the highest compliment paid to a hostess. What she does comes out of what she is herself, but she forgets herself completely. Her only thought is the comfort and ease of her guests. This lady was, I suppose, a volunteer. She gave herself and her time and expected nothing in return, but she smiled and brought to that dark place an unexpected shining.

An old man waiting for his treatment called the rambunctious little boy over and began to do tricks with pennies for him. Soon the mother was smiling, others were watching as the boy's face lit up with surprise and delight.

It came to me then that what made that room shine was the action of grace. "If I make my bed in hell," wrote the psalmist, "behold, Thou art there." That hospital had seemed to me the vestibule of hell an hour earlier. But behold, God was there—in the lady in green, in the nurse who by her touch brought comfort and courage, in the couple whose love showed through, in the man doing tricks.

Grace is a marvelous but elusive word. "Unmerited favor" is the definition most of us know. It means self-giving, too, and springs from the person's own being without condition or consideration of whether the object is deserving. Grace may be unnoticed. But there are usually some who will notice. "Where sin abounded, grace did much more abound," wrote St. Paul. And those who are in a desperation of suffering will notice it, will notice even its lightest touch, and will hold it a precious, an incalculably valuable thing.

Twelve Baskets of Crumbs

JOYCE GRENFELL, the British comedienne, does a monologue of a nursery school teacher explaining the day's activities to a visitor.

"This is my friend Caroline," she lilts, "and Caroline's painting such a lovely red picture, aren't you, Caroline? Let's see what it is. Perhaps it's a sunset, is it? Or an orange, but now that you tell me, I can see—it's Mummy. Aren't you going to give her any nose? No nose. I think it's so interesting the way they see things, don't you, Mrs. Hingle?"

The way they see things. It is interesting indeed. Nobody but Caroline would see Mummy as a noseless orange scribble, but then nobody else's relationship to Mummy exactly duplicates Caroline's. Who we are determines to some degree what we see, and none of us often sees a thing whole. We see rather one side of an issue, one angle of a building (where we stand affects our view), and only certain facets of a personality.

It is what makes a personality that has absorbed me a great deal lately—no, not what makes it but what we see of it, for it is made of far more than we see. Letters have been pouring in to me from all kinds of people who have known and been affected by one personality. He was my husband and finally, after a long battle with cancer, he lost the fight. I read over the medical reports—phrases like "patient extremely apprehensive, lethargic, pale"; "white 64-year-old male, very ill-appearing, but gives a coherent history"; "This man is an example of one who does not have what it takes to contain malignant disease . . . increasingly depressed, somewhat obtunded, wracked with pain."

It was doctors, of course, who saw him thus. Who they were determined what they saw. It was their business to see it. But had "squamous cells" and "adino-carcinoma" anything really to do with the man himself? They certainly played their part in destroying him —destroying the man whom the letters I was receiving called "a prince," "a true scholar with a ready but kindly wit and a beautiful sense of words," "the best boss I ever had."

The story of the feeding of the five thousand came to me because I found that I was dealing with fragments. "Gather up the fragments that remain," Jesus told his disciples, "that nothing be lost."

I wonder what they did with those twelve baskets of crumbs. Did they feed more people, or the same people again, or did they give them to dogs or pigs? We aren't told. But Jesus' sense of order prompted him to have them collected, and surely he had some purpose. They were bits of the real, original stuff. They were what was left over after the primary purpose had been fulfilled, but there was some use for them.

This is how it seems to me now. I am left with fragments, pieces of the real, original stuff (although the best is gone), and I cannot help gathering them up somehow "that nothing be lost."

There are his things. What do you do with the golf clubs, the drawer full of press notices, the tee shirts, the jacket with "Muskingum College" across the back, the beautiful sport coats, the Cambridge academic robes and diploma, the leather wallet with his name embossed on it, the monogrammed ring, the neckties, the luggage? You give some of it away, hoping that people will be able to fathom that you are giving them some of him.

76

Then there are the letters. Is anything more a part of a man than his handwriting? His hand rested on that page, and his mind was at work as his hand moved across it, putting down words that were the express image of his person. There are notebooks filled with marvelously thought out outlines of speeches made at men's dinners, ladies' luncheons, college commencements, cornerstone-layings, inaugurations and ordinations. There are outlines of sermons, outlines of books, complete lectures on courses he taught such as Theology and the Great Classics, Church and State, Martin Luther. A single word, underlined with a squiggly line, sometimes sufficed to remind him of a joke or an illustration and the outlines are full of these.

There are photographs: a curly-headed boy with his sister, a young man with slicked-down hair playing a saxophone, a football team, a line-up of lifeguards in bathing suits, a man in the Pentagon pulpit, a professor with his class, a father with his family, a man with his friends. This was his life.

Best of all to me are the articles and speech transcriptions. They are complete in themselves, but at the same time they are only fragments of the man.

You can't help forming some idea of a man who would entitle his columns "How to Kill a Polar Bear," "Dare to Be a Barnabas," "Ye Olde Thyme Religion," "Who Is This Gashmu?" "Tennyson, Anyone?" or "Achilles Was No Heel." He took a light view of himself, and Carlyle (I think) says somewhere that what a man is includes what others think of him and what he thinks of himself; both have some bearing on what he actually becomes. My husband is glimpsed, in his miscellaneous writings, driving fenceposts to keep in the steers he was hoping to make some money on; passing the time of night with another volunteer as they watched airplanes during World War II; sharing camaraderie with a truck driver after they rescued a "fat and faint lady" from a second story window during the Pittsburgh flood; fiddling with shower faucets vainly trying to produce an endurable water temperature. He could not stomach men who took themselves very seriously for very long.

Yet the fragments show that Addison Leitch was a man of deadly serious purpose. He knew that into his hands had been committed the ministry of the very Word of Life, the Word that is God, and it was his calling to commit it in turn to faithful men. There are tapes of his sermons and Bible studies in which Christ is always exalted, his grace always emphasized. But the voice is natural and vigorous, never tinged with what Spurgeon called the "ministerial tone."

It is out of the question for us to collect the crumbs "that nothing be lost." When a man dies it seems that nearly everything is lost, but that is not true. Hundreds, perhaps even thousands, have been fed.

And although we have but fragments of a life, although we know even ourselves only in a fragmented way, eternity has been written in our hearts, and the pieces will one day be put together exactly as they were meant to go. In Christ, we are told, "all things consist" (hold together) . . . The one who arranged to feed five thousand people, made them sit down in rows and saw to the gathering up of the leftovers, is still in charge. There is no fragmentation to him. He sees perfectly the details as well as the destinies of our lives, and orders them all in beauty and in love. They are, as Gerard Manley Hopkins wrote, "Far with fonder a care (and we, we should have lost it) finer, fonder a care kept."

*   *   *

Now that some time has passed, I am still unable to think of anything I particularly like about being a widow but there is one thing which the experience gives you, and that is perspective on marriage. I have recently been asked to speak to groups of students from this perspective, and I could go on and on. There is so much I would like to say to those who are thinking about getting married, though I know there won't be many in the audience who will actually do anything about what I say. They will listen—it is amazing how insatiable the hunger seems to be to hear somebody talk about marriage (and apparently all ages are hungry)—but a speaker can't say very much in 40 minutes, and of what he says little will be remembered and less will be acted upon.

A girl wrote to me from Chicago after attending a lecture and discussion group in which I had been questioned about cross-cultural marriage. I gave a brief answer, saying that I had no objection on ethical grounds to such a marriage, but that I did believe the risks were higher than they would otherwise be. The girl said in her letter that she was black and was very much interested in a black man from Kenya. She wanted me to spell out just what some of these risks might be. I thought about my reply for some time before sitting down to write to her, but realized then that the questions I was going to put down for her consideration did not differ from questions I would ask any young person who is contemplating marriage.

First, last and in-between, the most important requirement is companionability. Is this the man you want to spend the rest of your life with? The rest of your life? All sorts of people are interesting for a while. Lots of people are amusing and fun and the sort we want to meet at parties and do things with, but they're like New York City—"nice to visit but you wouldn't want to live there." Marriage is living there. It is what you come home to. It ought to be with the kind of person you'd want to run back to when you wanted to run away from everybody else.

I suggested a few other questions that might help the girl decide whether the man was companionable.

Is he:

punctual or habitually late? orderly or disorderly? a reader or a TV watcher? an outdoor man or an indoor man? a thinker or a talker?

Does he:

like your family? like your friends? have men friends? like to entertain, and would you be proud of him as a host? treat you like a woman? as you think a woman should be treated? have approximately the same education you have? come from a home similar to yours? like the kind of food you like to cook? read your kind of books? laugh at the same jokes you do?

Can you agree on:

sex? in-laws? children? money? religion? your respective roles in the home?

Of course there can't be any universally "right" and "wrong" answers to these questions. Your answers would probably tell a psychologist or a professional counselor some things about you, and I am sure the questions themselves without the answers would reveal a good many things about me that I may not be prepared for, but it seems to me they are good questions to use as a guide to sizing up how things may work out. For even to consider such matters as I have included here indicates a whole view of life and the world that a couple may find they either have or do not have in common.

I would not for a moment suggest that there are no happy marriages where one partner is orderly and the other disorderly. I have known couples who seemed quite happy knowing that one would always be late, and the other would always have to wait. Opposites often do seem to attract, and life is certainly more interesting where one complements the other. But it is possible for a marriage to bog down in the first week over the toothpaste tube—one turns out to be a squeezer and the other a twister, and unless the husband and wife have some deep unities which have drawn them together and some ultimate ends in common, even a toothpaste tube might undo them. For that will be only one of a thousand trivialities which are grains of sand in the bearings, and in a marriage based on nothing but trivialities (pure proximity, let's say—the bowling team, the sociology class, or what may for a while look much more significant, concurring views on racism or transactional analysis) there will be no way to clean the bearings.

My perspective of distance lets me look at my own experience of marriage, and at the marriages of others, and it is companionability every time which appears to me to be the secret of contentment. We all know couples who seem to "have everything"—they're both exceptionally good-looking and smart and talented and popular; they have two cute children and a beautiful house; he has a good job, and she is concerned and creative and sought-after by all the clubs and organizations who need a concerned and creative woman; but the marriage is a dead loss.

They're not companionable. They simply do not enjoy each other. Other women have a different perspective than the wife—they are sure they could enjoy a man like that and give him what he deserves. Other men think, "What else does he want? Wow!" But when the marriage finally ends on grounds of incompatibility everyone shakes his head and feels it's too bad, but incompatibility is incompatibility and there is nothing anybody can do about it.

There are many things which contribute to companionability or compatibility—things hinted at, I think, in the questions sent my correspondent. But if the answers give a favorable prognosis there is still one element I consider indispensable to being a true companion, and that is gratitude. Do we have any conception at all of the magnitude of the gift of a person to share our lives with? This real, live, breathing, thinking, loving man or woman to whom I have made such staggering promises in my marriage vows has given himself or herself to me. I get to live with him and share his life and he actually wanted me to share his life with him and here we are.

How often in a company of people when I have seen a wife contradict or belittle or ignore her husband I have wanted to leap from my chair, seize her by the shoulders and cry, "Do you realize what you've got?" Clearly she doesn't realize it just then. She's lost her perspective, lost the peculiar clarity of vision which the lover alone has for the beloved, and I know in my saner moments that nobody can keep it all the time. But there is nothing that will help us gain it back again like a little appreciation.

My husband used to say that if a wife wants to be very generous she may allow that her husband lives up to 80 percent of her expectations. She may, he said, choose to chip away at the other 20 percent (without reducing it by very much) till death them do part, or she may elect instead simply to enjoy the 80 percent she's got—enjoy it and thank God for it. How much more fun life will be for both of them if they elect to enjoy one another!

"For when all things were made," wrote Charles Kingsley, "none was made better than this: to be a lone man's companion, a sad man's cordial, a chilly man's fire . . . there is no herb like it under the canopy of heaven."

II

TO LEARN
AND TO TEACH

Confessions of a Teacher

A FEW MONTHS ago I made two short sallies into the field of teaching. One was an adult class sponsored on Tuesday evenings by a big city church. The other was a course in expression ("the presentation of ideas by speech, writing and behavior") on the graduate level. How salutary it would be for everyone who has to be taught if he could somehow, in the middle of the process, be required to teach. If he could be on the other side of the podium and, by trying to teach, learn how important is the attitude of the student toward the teacher.

I had some students who never looked at me. This bothered me immensely. I had some who seemed to be assiduously taking notes every minute and I was gratified, thinking it meant that in their opinion everything I said was worth taking down. Then it occurred to me that they might be writing letters or term papers for other professors. Some students looked at me the whole time. I could infer from this that they were enthralled by what I was saying, or (and how was I to tell the difference?) that nothing I said was worth taking a note on. Then there were some who encouraged me by looking up at the right times with an interested and even intelligent expression, and looking down at their notebooks when I had pronounced a particularly pithy and telling sentence.

My husband was a highly gifted and experienced

teacher and he was always profoundly affected by his students' attitudes and responses. It seemed to me when he told me this that he of all people ought not to bother about what his callow audience might think, but now I see that it was a measure of his humility and his dedication to the task. He called himself "a pointer and an explainer," rather than a scholar, and unless his students looked when he pointed and understood when he explained he had not done his job.

In the adult class in the city church there was a lady with a shopping bag. She was always there, never missed a class, always had the shopping bag which was always stuffed, and she always came up to speak to me either before or after the class. She would start right in without introduction on whatever was on her mind.

"I said to the Lord, 'Lord, you know I never liked the Book of Job. I never wanted to read it. Stayed away from it.' But honey girl, that's all changed now. I think I'm beginning to understand it. Not afraid of it anymore. This class has helped me. It's helped me with a lot of things. You know my son—the one that's in the mental hospital. Well, something's going to happen there. I know it is. I said to the Lord, 'I don't know what you're going to do but you're going to do something. It's going to be all right.' "

"But you didn't find that out in my class."

"Oh no. Listen—I study for this class. The Lord helps me. I went upstairs to my sister's. I live on the first floor but I went upstairs to her place and I said, 'Look, can I study here? I can't study in my own house.' See, I haven't got room. If you could see my place! I have books, I have magazines, I have puzzles, I have games. Oh dear. They're all over. Even the kitchen table. There's no place to sit down and write. I said to the Lord, 'One of these days, Lord, you're going to help me get this place cleaned out,' but I went upstairs to my sister's and she said, 'Go ahead, sit right down here and do your homework.' And I'm not kidding you, honey girl, it's wonderful what I learn. I think I'm a lot like that man Job. I said to the Lord, 'You've got another Job here, Lord.' He understands me. He knows what I'm talking about."

I was glad he did, for we had quite a number of conversations like this and the more she talked the less I understood. She rode home at night after the class alone on the subway. ("Senior Citizens ride for a dime," she told me, holding out the dime in her calloused little palm.) "Aren't you afraid to ride alone at night?" I asked. "No. The only thing I'm afraid of is sin." I guess she thought she wasn't likely to run into much of that on the subway.

Another student in the same class was an attorney—an attorney, in fact, whose client I had been. It is one thing to stand up in front of a hundred and twenty-five people for the first time and dish out the lesson you have prepared. You don't know who they are, they don't know you, and you have to let the chips fall where they may. But when they begin to emerge as faces and personalities and lives, the teacher begins to recognize his place as an instrument of truths much greater than himself, a servant of people who like Job himself stand alone before God, people whose ash heaps the teacher doesn't know anything about. How was I to interpret the Book of Job, "one of the colossal cornerstones of the world," as G.K. Chesterton called it, to the lawyer as well as to the lady who rode the subway from her cluttered apartment, clutching her bulging shopping bag, and traveling in-between-times up to the state hospital to visit her 38-year-old son?

There was less variety in the members of the class on expression. They were all seminary students, and there were only twenty-eight of them. But I found out after the first assignment, which was to write a two-page autobiography, that they would be too much for me. I wanted to teach them about writing and the making of distinctions and language and courtesy and sensibility and sexuality and order, and I knew I had better not pull any punches. Along the way I tried to get them to stop using *like* as a conjuction and *hopefully* to mean "I hope that" and *momentarily* to mean "in a moment" instead of "for a moment" (and airline pilots aren't helping in this at all, because on every flight they announce over the intercom that "we will be taking off momentarily"). I shouted at them and stamped my feet to try to get them to stop using *Reverend* without the definite article, or as a form of direct address, and to get them to spell and pronounce *sacrilegious* correctly instead of as though it were somehow related to the word religious, and on the final examination they gave me sentences like, "Looks like it's going to rain," "Hopefully it won't rain," "Your visitor will be here momentarily, sir," and "Reverend Brown preached a lengthy sermon." I wanted to go out and hang myself.

Then I rememberd my husband's often repeated advice, "Remember you're nothing but a seed-sower. Just sow the seed." And words of a teacher far greater than Add Leitch, "He that hath ears to hear let him hear." Not many in a given audience will have ears to hear. You can teach some of the people some of the time.

And I thought of things that have dawned on me after forty years, things others have tried to get me to see which I didn't see, things I have read again and again and then, strangely, on the seventeenth reading, light breaks through. "O fools, and slow of heart to believe!"

I wondered, when I read my students' examination papers, whether I had perhaps been overly ambitious in what I attempted to cover in eleven weeks. My fears were somewhat allayed when I came across the description of a course called "Problems of Human Behavior" offered in a California junior college. According to the catalogue, the course covered:

"Science, the 'easy rider' effect, society, psychology, group behavior, free will, determinism, controls, utopia, maturation, conformity, meaning, communication, culture, individual personal behavior, anthropology, punishment, people gap, love, discrimination, war, peace, cold war, defense, politics, aggression, God, religion, church, Jesus, family, marriage, sex, happiness, drugs, mass media, patriotism, Communism, socialism, capitalism, pollution, deviant behavior, mercy killing, abortion, birth control, civil disorders, freedom, independence, leadership, heroes, the draft, military, education, grades, teachers, racism, minorities, violence, and other important issues."

Me overly ambitious in what I attempted to cover in my course? My efforts were sheer poltroonery compared with that junior college professor's. While one would certainly have to hand it to him for pluck in tackling such an array, one could ask a lot of questions about a course like that (in what sense, for instance, may science, peace, heroes and teachers be classified as "problems of human behavior"?) and about the institution that includes it in its curriculum (is it one of those where students rather than faculty plan the curriculum?) and about whatever happened to old-fashioned problems like anger and jealousy and avarice. And what about the frame of reference? What sort of professor could profess to deal with the material of that course unless he knew of a firm foundation, unless he believed there was someone in charge? Or are we all languishing on an ash heap, buffeted by whirlwinds from which no Voice speaks?

If I am given the chance again to teach I will, at the risk of sounding irrelevant, still refuse to take my cues from this century's god, "The Mass Media." I will refuse to define all of life in terms of "problems" or my hopes in terms of "solutions," and I will talk again about suffering and language and courtesy and order. I will continue publishing my belief that there is a God who has entered into a covenant relationship with his people, ordered in all things and sure.

Getting Back to Nature

THERE IS SOMETHING which seems to me a little bit touching about the spectacle of Americans getting back to nature. I understand the urge. I love the outdoors, I love hiking, mountain climbing, picnicking. I lived for six years on a wooded hillside in the White Mountains, and although we live in a suburb now we are glad that we have nearly two acres of land, including two nice stands of evergreen trees and an overgrown field. But we don't have a backyard barbecue and we don't go camping.

My daughter was 8 years old when she first spent a summer in the United States, and she wanted to know why we never went camping. I tried to explain. What did she think we had been doing all her life? We had lived in the forest of Ecuador, part of the time in leaf-roofed shacks, always cooking over a wood fire, traveling (when we weren't in an airplane) by foot and canoe, quite often eating what the Indians gave us.

"No, I mean real camping," she said, meaning the kind Americans do so frantically as soon as warm weather comes. Now that we've spent thousands of years getting ourselves civilized so that we can live away from the weather, cook indoors and get food from a store instead of having to hunt, gather or plant it, we go to any lengths to "rough it" again.

All we need nowadays in order to get back to nature is a few thousand dollars' worth of equipment to haul along the nation's million-dollar highways. A station wagon will do, with a trailer on the back, a trailer which contains perhaps a boat, a trailbike or a house—a self-contained house, which contains in miniature everything our year-round house contains, or a canvas house called a tent with which we need pressure stoves and canned fuel or charcoal stoves with packaged bricquets and lighter fluid; pressure lamps, chemical toilets, plastic sinks with self-contained water storage, folding aluminum cots with vinyl webbing or foam rubber pads, synthetic-filled sleeping bags (or disposable sleeping bags such as Sears advertises this season), mosquito netting, insect repellent, dehydrated, all-in-one-package pre-cooked meals, and a few hundred dollars' worth of hunting and fishing gear for the man who needs to hunt and fish, not in order to eat but in order to get away from the family who is getting away from civilization.

I am touched when I see the American family tooling along the interstate with all of this—the Kleenex box visible in the front window, the kids' bare feet sticking out the back window, the baby in the nylon net playpen, the lunch in the styrofoam chest, and the mother with her hair in plastic rollers because this is the night they're going to eat in a restaurant so she won't have to cook outdoors.

I remember (forgive me, but I can't help it) the kind of camping we did. Not that we had a choice. We lived in the jungle with Indians, and to go anywhere or do anything with them meant doing it their way whether or not Val admitted that this was real camping. Their gear: a gun and a few shells, an aluminum cooking pot and some matches (no dishes—they used leaves; no spoons—they used their fingers), a machete, a bottle of salt and a thin blanket. If there was a canoe they carried in it a head of plantains and some manioc. In the bow of the canoe was a pottery shard with a small fire burning to keep away some of the gnats.

There are young people who are turned off by the usual American way of getting back to nature and they have been trying what looks to them like a more authentic way. Communal life looks like the real thing, and thousands have left towns and cities for places like New Mexico where they can start again, as they like to think, simply and honestly. The Chicanos who live in New Mexico don't see it that way. They see it as a mockery of everything they've been doing to try to earn a respectable niche in the American scene.

A national picture magazine recently carried an article on one of these experiments. It started out with a description of singing and dancing in the twilight in the vicinity of a bonfire—something the writer called "shared orgasmic warmth" but which sounded to me like Indian Night at a boy's summer camp. The members of this particular commune, the article said, had come to these remote mountains and mesas "hoping for a home," spurred on by "an urge to get out of their own skins."

I know that urge. It's a dream of Utopia and being human we all have those dreams. Life gets terribly chilly, sometimes, and complicated, and we long for warmth, for simplicity, for love, even before we have learned what those words mean, let alone what they are going to cost, and we somehow hope that by giving up a lot of things (things which have perhaps been given to us by people who have worked very hard for them, or things which have been developed over the centuries by the world's finest minds, or things people have actually died for) we can get back to Eden.

What the magazine story showed so clearly, and what I suppose many people in communes don't see so clearly just yet, is that getting back to Nature, unless you are going to go back by yourself, means getting back to human nature all over again, which means starting from scratch with the same problems the Establishment was established to alleviate, and, ultimately, working our way all the way up again to the things we had decided to get away from.

First off, the people in the communes found that they had to have some capital. Luckily an "affluent hip-type" came across with $50,000, so they had something to buy a tractor and some tools with. (It was lucky, too, that somewhere, somehow, that tractor had been designed and constructed and was for sale.)

Then they found they had to have some authority. Not a head man, really, but a man named Justin (over 30) who because he had been there the longest (and presumably had experience which presumably had taught him something the rest didn't know) sort of helped people know that they were supposed to do.

Then they wanted some sort of religion. Not directed to any particular god, of course—no need for doctrines or creeds or anything like that—but, as one man put it, "I dig the idea of saying grace—just 'Bless this food'— you know?" So they joined in something that looked like prayer.

They lived in tepees for a time but it can be cold in New Mexico and they felt the need of better shelter. What do you build a house out of in the wilds of the Southwest? Fortunately some neighboring Chicano showed them—adobe bricks. There were members of the group who had been to college, or who knew how to play guitars, or who rode motorcycles. But Justin said, "Maybe making abode bricks isn't your own thing, but you make it your thing if you live here." The idea sounds close to a contract.

The big house was all right for a while. It kept the rain off and the cold out better than the tepees did, but there were people inside, and it began to seem to some of them that there were too many people for one room and they began adding private rooms. As they ex-

94

plained, "Every man needs some sort of sphere of autonomy." Hmm.

What about rules? Many people are sick of rules. They don't want anybody telling them what to do. A commune is a place where rules aren't needed, surely. But in the outhouse in this place in New Mexico there's a big sign, DID YOU CLOSE THE LID? Somebody had thought up the idea of sanitation—the outhouse, to begin with, and then a rule to govern its use.

The system seems to be working so far. They have some food, they have shelter, they have learned to mend the clothes they came in, and those who stay have found ways of getting along together. Is it self-supporting? Well, almost. But there is a subsidy, which is nice. Where the love and goodwill of the members turn out to be not quite enough they fall back on "love money." This means money earned "outside" on farms (farms which are the backbone of the Establishment— that kind of farm?), or given by relatives and friends who work at regular jobs—those who haven't yet discovered the simple life.

Maybe we needn't point out to these hopeful kids just what it is they're up to. Maybe we don't need to quote to them the words of the Preacher in Ecclesiastes, "There's nothing new under the sun." Maybe we shouldn't ask them to think of the past and all they owe to it, to their parents, their country, to God. Surely they'll see it themselves one of these days. But perhaps a long, cool look would help some of us who gaze so wistfully at those Edens. We cannot go back.

But we can go on. And it takes faith—the kind that accepts all that has gone into making us what we are and hopes for what God has promised us. Paul wrote to the Roman Christians, "Let God remold your minds from within, so that you may prove in practice that the plan of God for you is good, meets all his demands, and moves toward the goal of true maturity."

Some of My Best Friends Are Books

I HAVE ALMOST ALWAYS been surrounded by books. I wouldn't be surprised if my mother put some in the crib along with my toys, just to get me used to them early. The first house I remember living in was one of those double ones of which there are hundreds in the suburbs of Philadelphia. We lived in Germantown, in what was probably a cramped house (although to me as a child it seemed large) and there were books in the living room, books in the dining room, books in all of the bedrooms and tall bookcases lining the halls. My father came home at night with a briefcase full of papers and books.

Before I could read much myself I looked at picture books, like everybody else. I remember the lovely women and elegantly handsome men in Charles Dana Gibson's book of drawings. I went back again and again to an animal book which had a horrifyingly hideous photo of an angry gorilla with teeth bared. The beautiful little pictures in Beatrix Potter's books of neatly furred small animals gave me a delicious feeling of order and comfort. My mother read these aloud to me, and how eagerly I stooped with Lucie to enter Mrs. Tiggywinkle's laundry; or accompanied Simpkin the cat as he made his way through Gloucester's snowy lanes. Mr. MacGregor was a big, bad bogeyman to me. Mother read, too, the Christopher Robin stories, and I found myself identifying her with Kanga, my older brother Phil with Pooh, Dave with Piglet, and myself, alas but inescapably with Eeyore.

Evenings at home were often spent with the whole family sitting together, each with his head in a book. Or at times my father would read aloud. He bored us to death reading passages from Jonathan Edwards, George Whitefield, or George Borrow. *The Bible in Spain* was "good writing," he said, and he wanted us to hear it. He loved good writing, and as an editor had to read an awful lot of appallingly bad writing, but I am grateful now for his efforts to teach us the difference. He also read sometimes to us from Henry A. Shute's *Real Diary of a Real Boy,* which got the closest thing to a belly laugh I ever heard out of my sedate father.

A big dictionary was always within reach of the dining room table because it was there that arguments most frequently arose over words. He wanted them quickly settled, and made us look up the words in question.

A part of each summer was spent at "The Cottage," a big old lodge-type house in the White Mountains built by my great-great uncle, who was, among other things, editor of the *New York Journal of Commerce* and a writer of books. His bedroom on the second floor, an enormous paneled one with a huge fireplace, had hardly been rearranged at all since he died, and one wall was still lined with crumbling leather-bound books. A rainy day in the mountains was a chance for me to pore over field manuals from the Civil War, great volumes on law, Mrs. Oliphant's novels, or a tiny set, tinily printed, of the unabridged *Arabian Nights.*

There were magazines on the bottom shelves, too— old ones, with advertisements of Pear's Soap or Glen kitchen ranges, and I found in them serialized stories by Robert Louis Stevenson.

The first full-length book I recall reading was not a

piece of great literature, but it had a great effect on my malleable mind. It was called *Hell on Ice,* the saga of sixty men who attempted to reach the North Pole by way of the Bering Strait. Only a few survived, and I agonized with them as they froze and starved on the icy wastes. I was carried out of myself and my pleasant porch hammock into danger, suffering and death. I became aware of vulnerability, mortality and human courage.

To my detriment I managed to go through four years of high school without reading more than two or three classics. I had a good freshman English teacher who made me see vividly the world of chivalry and heraldry through *Ivanhoe,* so that I still love to visit the medieval halls of museums. In my junior or senior year I very hastily skimmed *David Copperfield* in order to write a book report. I may have read one or two others which I have entirely forgotten, but literature was merely a requirement. No other teacher made me understand what it was all about. (B.F. Westcott said, "It is the office of art to reveal the meaning of that which is the object of sense.")

But of course there was the Bible, in a class all by itself. This was The Book in our home, and we heard it read every day, usually twice a day. The King James English was as simple and familiar to me, with all its "beholds" and "it came to passes" as Philadelphia talk (pronounced twawk). The resonance of the books of Moses, the cadences of the Psalms, the lucidity of the Gospel of John, the soaring rhapsodies of Paul on the love of God, the strange figures of the Book of the Revelation, all sank deeply into my heart and mind. Everything in life, I believed, had meaning as it related to what I knew of The Book.

There were many books in our home by and about people who lived by the Bible. It was in Amy Carmichael, a missionary to South India, that I found the kind of woman I wanted to be. She was at work for the Lord (an Anglican, she had founded a place for saving little girls from temple prostitution) and she took time in the midst of this to write of her experience as she walked by faith in a place where almost no one shared that faith.

A friend gave me *The Imitation of Christ* when I was in college, and I read it slowly, finishing it the following summer during evenings in a university stadium where I climbed up to watch the sunset.

One year when I was tutoring I came across, in the library of my pupils, a dull-looking novel called *Salted with Fire*. I had never heard of George MacDonald, but his writing gave me a whole new vista of the love of God. There was a shining quality to it, and a deep humanity. C.S. Lewis, I later learned, had found it too, and did an anthology of MacDonald's work.

The biographies of missionaries—Hudson Taylor of China, James Fraser of Lisuland, David Brainerd of early New Jersey, Raymond Lull of North Africa—influenced the course of my life. Sometimes, if we can catch the sound of music that other people march to, we can fall into step.

It was when I lived in the jungle that books were hard to keep. Mold, mildew, crickets and smoke did their worst, and I did not always have a way to transport more than one or two books at a time, nor a place to keep them other than an Indian carrying net hung under the thatch. But they became even more precious, more indispensable in times when I had little contact with English-speaking people. I got around to reading some great books then—Tolstoy's *Anna Karenina,* Teilhard de Chardin's *The Divine Milieu,* Isak Dinesen's *Out of Africa.* Each spoke to me in some powerful, personal way.

Kafka said that books should serve as "the axe for the frozen sea within us." Tolstoy showed me my own vulnerability and need of redemption—as Flannery O'Connor does, too, in her "stories about original sin," as she describes them. De Chardin illuminated for me the immanence of God. Dinesen reveals majesty and dignity in human beings and animals as creatures of God, and the laughter at the heart of things. (In one book, *Seven Gothic Tales,* she touches the courage of the Creator, the power of women, a herd of unicorns, the reason for seasons, the dogs of God, angels and chamber pots, coffee and the word of the Lord, and Mary Magdalene on Good Friday Eve. Imagine the humor and courage it takes to put all that in seven stories!)

A reader understands what he reads in terms of what he is. As a Christian reader I bring to bear on the book I am reading the light of my faith. "All things are yours, for ye are Christ's, and Christ is God's," said Paul. Browning's Fra Lippo Lippi expresses it this way:

> "... *This world's no blot for us, nor blank;*
> *It means intensely, and means good:*
> *To find its meaning is my meat and drink."*

Return to Order

"SERENDIPITY" is in a class with words like "share," "meaningful," and "creative" in my mind—they are words I try at all costs to avoid. But I suppose it has its place since it's in the dictionary now as a word that Horace Walpole coined in his story, "Three Princes of Serendip." Now Serendip is bad enough as another name for Ceylon, but I am sure I would not have liked "Ceylonity" any better than serendipity as a name for an apparent aptitude for making fortunate discoveries accidentally. I don't have that aptitude myself.

Nobody is going to say that meeting up with famous people twice inside of a week amounts to an aptitude, but whatever it amounts to I want to put down here that I rode on a plane with Ike and Tina Turner and their singing group, and heard them sing (*sotto voce* in the back of the plane) "Bringing in the Sheaves." ("How'd you learn that?" one of them asked. "Guess we all went to the same church!" was the reply.) And only a few days later I found myself standing, in an empty and silent parking garage late at night in Boston, next to Flip Wilson. We were both at the cashier's desk and I had the temerity to ask for his autograph. Very graciously he wrote on a piece of paper "Don't fight the feelin'" and signed it "Geraldine." ("Oh," said a friend of mine when he heard about it, "You got his autograph for your daughter." "No, for myself." Astonished stare.)

I got two happy surprises out of a recent news magazine. One was a picture of neatly dressed students. They were applying for jobs and this was to them an adequate reason for dressing neatly. The ordinary courtesy which requires a person to groom himself for the sake of the rest of us seems an inadequate reason to many.

The same magazine told about a school in California where they teach a no-nonsense curriculum grounded in the three Rs. "Parents are fed up with violence, vandalism, poor teaching and permissiveness," a board member was quoted as saying. "They want their kids to be disciplined and to learn the basics—how to count, spell, read and write."

I hope these are signs of a return to order.

I never knew that there is a desert in the middle of the state of Washington until last month when a group of students asked me to come out there. I flew out on one of those very rare days when the national weather-map indicated clear weather from coast to coast. The weathermen were right. It was such a glorious sight to see the U.S.A. unrolled beneath us that I put away my book and watched the hills of Massachusetts and New York, the checkerboard fields of Ohio and Indiana in newly-ploughed and newly-planted brown and green, the vast cornfields of Illinois and Iowa, and then, after we had crossed the Missouri River near Pierre, South Dakota, I puzzled over the strange terrain below, all of it beige, pale beige, with black squiggles which I concluded must be water. Not round ponds as in the east, but threadworm squiggles in the humpy, utterly empty landscape. Very few houses or cultivated fields were visible—not even many roads. We crossed the wrinkled Rockies, the Yellowstone River, the Grand Tetons, and then I began to puzzle in earnest. I saw perfectly round discs set like huge coasters or doilies in totally barren areas. I could not tell what the discs were, but because they were bright green or dark brown in contrast to the beige around them, I knew they must be planted fields. But why circular?

When I was being driven from Pasco, Washington, to a place called Wanapum, I learned about those discs. They are called central pivot irrigation, and may be planted to anything from sugar beets to potatoes or wheat. An arm as much as a quarter of a mile long (a quarter of a *mile!*) is rotated with a built-in sprinkler system so that a disc half-a-mile in diameter is irrigated continuously. Marvelous. Who thought of it? Why didn't somebody think of it sooner? How did they figure out that they could make it so long? But it was done, and it brought order out of chaos, and where there had been only sage and tumbleweed there were now these neat, satisfying contiguous circles, bringing forth all manner of living, edible things.

And then there was Wanapum. A town of twenty houses (I counted them), without a store or gas station, set near a huge dam on the Columbia River, surrounded by sage and tumbleweed and high bare brown mountains. A conference? Here? But they told me there would be five hundred students!

There were. They came from Washington and from Oregon and from California and even from Missouri and Maryland. They brought tents and sleeping bags and set up their little individual camps on the grass or in the classrooms of the school which the government had built for the people of the town but which had never been used because it turned out to be cheaper to bus pupils to the next town than to run the school. They gave me a trailer all to myself and although it rocked in the winds which whipped down through the Columbia gorge I discovered to my utter delight that it had among its few conveniences an electric blanket.

103

There were blue jeans everywhere and many guitars and more clapping and singing than I have ever heard and the walls of the gym were decked with banners about Jesus made by various chapters of a group called "Seekers," and I wondered what I could possibly have to say to these eager people that would make it worth their while to transport me from the east coast for a conference of less than 48 hours. I had no striking spiritual novelties to offer. I tried simply to take them back to a few eternal verities. Our own souls are in confusion. The reality of God in Christ brings order.

"Oh no," one girl told me she had said to herself when I started to talk, "No, she can't *talk* to these kids like that. She'll make them *hate* her." But they listened and from what they said I knew that they didn't hate me, and they asked for more. When I talked to women about God's order in creation and the place of women in the divine hierarchy they seemed hungry to hear it, glad to know there are guidelines and limits and rules within which we find our true freedom. "What a relief to hear!" said one, and "like a fresh breeze," said another—and a man at that.

I was cheered to find this eagerness for discipline and discipleship. I was even cheered by the knowledge that several classrooms had been set aside for women who actually wanted to sleep at night instead of talk, and I heard next day that those classrooms were packed. Is it a whole new direction for students to opt for the sensible, the ordered? I hope so.

A black couple stayed with me a few weeks ago. Both teach in a private school on Long Island, and they are trying to introduce some respect for authority and order in their (mostly white) classes. And the kids are learning. They call them "Sir" and "Ma'am," and they catch on very fast to what is required. The whole idea that certain things are *required* in this school and are not optional and that students must do them or else is a new one to some, but it's amazing how it works. This couple is very young and therefore very sympathetic to the views of youth, but they are also very Christian and determined that their students learn that there is a total view of life and the world at stake here, a view that understands true liberty as obedience to a divine order.

Martha Graham's understanding of ballet may not spring from a Christian perspective at all, but it is interesting that long years of experience—plain hard work, gruelling work—have taught her that, according to a *New Yorker* article, "freedom, to a dancer, means only one thing: discipline." And is there any image of human freedom more thrilling than a floating, spinning ballerina, or a springing, soaring dancer?

The *National Geographic*'s article "The Incredible Universe" (May 1974) says, "Imagine that the thickness of this page represents the distance from the earth to the sun (93 million miles, or about 8 light minutes). Then the distance to the nearest star (4 1/3 light years) is a 71-foot-high stack of paper . . . while the edge of the known universe is not reached until the pile of paper is 31 million miles high." "The work of Thy fingers," said the psalmist. Can we put our puny lives into that strong hand, or submit our wills to the mind of such a Maker?

Within the ordered universe there seems also to be a unity before unimagined. Recent experiments show how plants are affected by the treatment they get from human beings, how one plant actually cringes when another in its vicinity is damaged, how a mother rabbit reacts each time one of her babies is drowned miles away. All creation groans.

A doctor friend of mine took me to visit a medical school. In one laboratory were jars containing babies—not the expected fetuses in various stages of development, but full-term human beings in whom things had gone hideously wrong. One coiled little white body, apparently normal in every other way, had two heads. I stood appalled.

"It is easy to be both sentimental and theological over the more agreeable and charming aspects of nature," wrote Evelyn Underhill, that twentieth-century saint who saw so much so clearly. "It is very difficult to see its essential holiness beneath disconcerting and hostile appearances with an equable and purified sight; with something of the large, disinterested charity of God."

God is not yet finished with his work. We are unfinished souls; his world is marred and bleared with suffering. But the hand that held the seven stars in the book of the Revelation is the hand that is laid on us as it was on John, and it is the voice that sounded like thunder and like a giant waterfall that speaks those quiet words, "Fear not. I am the First and the Last. I died . . . I am alive . . . I have the keys."

Flesh Becomes Word

ISAK DINESEN in *Out of Africa* tells how she was sometimes asked to sit in on a Kyama, an assembly of the elders of the farm, authorized by the government to settle local differences among the squatters. After a certain shooting accident she had to write out a statement, dictated by a man named Jogona Kanyagga, regarding events leading up to the accident and proving his own right to claim the victim as his son. When the long tale was told (during which Jogona sometimes had to break off, hold his head in both hands and gravely slap the crown of it "as if to shake out the facts") the baroness read it back to him. As she read out his own name, she writes, "he swiftly turned his face to me, and gave me a great fierce flaming glance, so exuberant with laughter that it changed the old man into a boy, into the very symbol of youth. Such a glance did Adam give the Lord when he formed him out of the dust, and breathed into his nostrils the breath of life and man became a living soul. I had created him and shown him himself, Jogona Kanyagga of life everlasting. When I handed him the paper, he took it reverently and greedily, folded it up in a corner of his cloak and kept his hand upon it. He could not afford to lose it, for his soul was in it, and it was the proof of his existence . . . the flesh was made word."

Words are inadequate, we say. So they often are. But they are nonetheless precious. "A word fitly spoken is like apples of gold in pictures of silver." In a time of

107

crisis we learn how intensely we need both flesh and word. We cannot do well without either one. The bodily presence of people we love is greatly comforting, and their silent companionship blesses us. "I know I can't say anything that will help, but I wanted to come," someone says, and the word they would like to speak is spoken by the coming. Those who can't come send instead of their presence, word. A letter comes, often beginning, "I don't know what to say," but it is an expression, however inadequate, of the person himself and what he feels toward us.

Before Eve heard the voice of the serpent summoning her to the worst possibility of her being, before Adam heard the voice of God summoning him to his best, the Word was. The Word was at the beginning of things, the Word was with God, the Word was God. That Word became invisible in the flesh when the man Christ came to earth. Man saw him, talked with him, learned from him, and when his flesh was glorified and he returned once more to his Father, men declared what they had seen. "That which was from the beginning, which we have heard, which we have seen with our eyes, which we have looked upon and touched with our hands concerning the word of life . . . we proclaim also to you." That eternal Word had become flesh and through those who knew Christ that flesh had become once more Word. Those who hear that Word today and believe it begin to live it and again it becomes flesh.

If I had a choice, I would not want to do without either the word or the flesh. I want letters from my friends, but I want to see their faces. I see them, but then I want them to say something. I have a guest book in which I always ask people to write their names, explaining that they need not write anything more unless they want to, but I open it after they are gone in hopes that they will have written some word as well.

"Say it with flowers," says the advertisement but when the flowers come how eagerly we look to see what the card says.

When I come to God I want words. Even though "there is not a word in my tongue but lo, O Lord, thou knowest it altogether," I want to say something to him. He knows what I look like, he knows my frame, remembers that I am dust. Does this flesh need words to speak to him. It does. There is, of course, a silence that waits on God. There is a lifting up of hands that takes the place of words. But there are times when we want desperately to speak. "Each in his own words" is all very well if you can find them, but often I find them only in the words of others.

I am troubled by the tendency today to assume that one's own words are "better" or more sincere than someone else's. The bizarre wording of wedding invitations I have received this year makes me want to go and hide rather than "share the joy." I did actually attend a wedding ceremony composed ("created" was what they called it) by the couple themselves, complete with prayers of their own making for the minister to read. This was somehow supposed to surpass the words of the Prayer Book. It didn't. Surely it is possible to repeat in all honesty expressions which others have found to be adequate which are at the same time both noble and beautiful? Doesn't it draw one out of himself, beyond his own horizons, to participate in an ancient ceremony? Does it really follow that the substitution of something "original" makes the thing richer?

Take the Psalms. They are human cries. Whoever wrote them knew the bottom of the barrel. He had felt his bones rot. He had sunk in slime, been ridden over, torn in two, betrayed, outraged and bludgeoned. He knew the sweeping barreness of loneliness, the forsakenness of grief, the bewilderment of unanswered prayer and put them all into words that speak to my condition. So I read them back to God—with the expressions of faith and praise that punctuate the howls. "My heart is in anguish within me . . . horror overwhelms me . . . he will deliver my soul in safety from the battle that I wage," (Psalm 55:4,5,18); "My wounds grow foul and fester because of my foolishness . . . but for thee, O Lord, do I wait. It is thou, O Lord, who wilt answer my prayer" (Psalm 38:5,15); "The earth reeled and rocked . . . but the Lord was my stay" (Psalm 18:7, 18).

How poor my own words would be compared to those of the Collect for Evening Prayer: "Lighten our darkness, we beseech thee, O Lord; and by thy great mercy defend us from all perils and dangers of this night; for the love of thy only Son Our Saviour Jesus Christ." I would be hard put to improve on Paul's prayer for the Roman Christians when I am praying for my friends (as an old lady in Canada used to pray for me, and included this prayer in nearly every letter she wrote me): "May the God of hope fill you with all joy and peace in believing, so that by the power of the Holy Spirit you may abound in hope."

Hymns are a powerful source of strength to me. Who of us can match words like William Williams' "Guide me, O thou great Jehovah, pilgrim through this barren land" or Henry Twell's "Thy touch hath still its ancient power; No word from thee can fruitless fall; Hear in this solemn evening hour, and in thy mercy heal us all"?

In the old words of George Herbert such as "Love bade me welcome, yet my soul drew back" or in the more modern poetry of Amy Carmichael: "And yet we come, Thy righteousness our cover, Thy precious blood our one, our only plea; And yet we come, O Savior,

Master, Lover—To whom, Lord, could we come, save unto Thee?" In such words my own flesh (empty, dumb, aching, needy as it may be) becomes, to God, word.

Spontaneity

A BOY OF TWO was standing in a bright square of sunlight in my kitchen one morning. He lifted his hands in the slanting ray that streamed through the open door. Then he lifted his face to me—a round, sweet face with a broad smile, lit with the sun and the light of discovery. "Look at these sunshine crumbs, Aunt Betty!" he said.

That was a spontaneous remark. Spontaniety may produce some delightful results, but for something to happen spontaneously it is necessary that certain conditions be present.

The little boy's observation does not arise "out of the blue," but from a personality which, even at two years of age, has already been shaped by his parents, where he lives, what he hears, how he is trained and treated.

His mind is ready and eager to receive impressions and searches at once for words to capture those impressions. His vocabulary is limited, but he knows sunshine, and he knows crumbs—so in a flash he has given a name to the thing he sees.

His fingers reach out and touch nothing. Crumbs you can touch. Sunshine crumbs, he finds, you can't touch. He has absorbed all this in a second and has made it forever his own, making it at the same time his Aunt Betty's.

I was in a laundromat one hot summer morning in Missouri. An old woman in a cotton dress, bobby socks and thick-soled shoes was doing her wash and greeted me cheerfully. We talked about the weather, and I told her I was from Massachusetts. When her husband came in she told him the lady was from Massachusetts, and he said the weather back East had been bad, hadn't it, and that he had been back East once.

"During the War. We was in Atlantic City, New Jersey, and they made us march on that boardwalk that goes along there by the ocean, you know that boardwalk. Well the guy in front of me—there was a little bitty patch o' ice on the boardwalk—and the guy in front of me when he come to that patch o' ice he fell right flat on his face. And we marched on down to the end of the boardwalk and turned around and marched back again and that guy fell flat on his face again when he come to that same little bitty patch o' ice."

That was the man's conversation, in its entirety. I thought about it for quite a while afterward. It always interests me to see just what it is that triggers people's remarks. Spontaneous action, the dictionary says, occurs, or is produced, within, of its own energy or force.

The old man's story, called to mind by the ideas of weather or of "back East," was spontaneous enough— not profound, of course, but the story and the images came out of the rich soil of his vivid experience.

Something had happened to him; his telling of it was straightforward. He wasn't concerned with the kind of impression he might be making on me. He was brief, and so clear that I'll never forget that scene during the war, the man himself, his wife or even the laundromat in that hot little town.

Spontaneous action may also mean "without pre-meditation," and this was true of what both the little boy and the old man said. Too often we are overly self-conscious; we play roles. Recently I saw a young man

113

on television whose performance did not delight me. It depressed me.

He said, "As opposed to for example in other words in terms of borrowing from a loan company you'd do better at a bank." He hadn't meditated much on that one. He was thinking about the setting, not about the subject.

The conditions which created his "spontaneity" were (1) the talk show format, where you have to talk, and you have to put on a show; (2) a time allotment, which means the poor man had to keep on talking without pausing to think what he was saying; and (3) the man himself—trained to value such meaningless phrases as "for example," "as opposed to," "in other words," and "in terms of" because he thinks they sound learned.

The man was also quite conscious of his own image in the TV monitors and had little leisure for looking clearly at the matter at hand as my nephew had looked at the dust flecks.

If spontaneity implies the existence of an inner energy to begin with, one felt that his energy had petered out by the time the man delivered his remark.

I'm being hard on him, and he was, as I have said, young. Carlyle wrote of 19-to-25-year-old youths that they had reached "the maximum of detestability." We have been telling ourselves that youth is beautiful and spontaneity one of the most beautiful things about youth. I wonder if spontaneity is not sometimes a euphemism for laziness—and indulgence which Carlyle found in youth. Isn't it much easier not to prepare one's mnd and heart, not to premeditate, simply to have things (O, vacuous word!) "unstructured"?

If you leave a thing altogether alone in hopes that it will happen all by itself, the chances are it never will. Who learns to play the piano, wins an election or loses weight spontaneously?

I have just read Jean Nidetch's book on the Weight Watchers, and while it is obvious that her basic theme (that people get fat because they eat) is hardly a world-shaking discovery, her method is one that made her a millionaire: get people to work at their problems together. Reducing doesn't just happen. It isn't a thing the majority succeed in doing all by themselves.

She doesn't let them make up their own diet as they go along—that's what put the fat on them in the first place. She doesn't suggest that losing weight is best done when you feel like it. She doesn't even say that it works only if you are being "yourself."

In fact I was reminded throughout the book of how many analogies there are between losing weight and practicing Christianity. There are rules to obey. Your *will* to obey them. Some people insist that the devotional life is somehow purer or better if it is pursued only when we feel like it. Worship for some is thought to be an "experience," rather than an act. Losing weight is also an experience—there's no doubt about that—in fact the expression "being born again" occurs in the testimonies of those who have done it. But losing weight most certainly has to begin with an act.

It is an act of the will. You decide to do *this* and not to do *that*. You must arrange, prepare and carefully carry out your plan. The combustion of those daily calories will happen without fail, but only when the conditions are properly set up.

Love is another thing. "But I want it to be spontaneous," people say. They think that if nothing is happening it is good enough reason for a divorce. "If it isn't spontaneous, it isn't love," they tell us. Where did that idea get started? Do we understand what spontaneity requires?

The kind of love the Bible talks about is action, and it comes from a force and an energy within. That energy is the love of Christ. His love creates the condition of heart (it does not come from nowhere) which enables us to do things: to give a cup of cold water, to go a second mile, to "look for a way of being constructive," as Phillips' translation puts I Corinthians 13:4. "It is, in fact, the one thing that still stands when everything else has fallen."

Christian love is a far cry from a misunderstood spontaneity which is merely unstructured. This love is a very firm and solid thing indeed, requiring will, obedience, action and an abiding trust in the "Strong Son of God, Immortal Love."

Speaking and Thinking:
First the Latter and Then the Former

ONE OF THE THINGS my husband Addison and I hoped we would have time to do was a book on *The Care and Feeding of Public Speakers*. Both of us had suffered many things at the hands of program chairmen, while often greatly blessed and cheered by being wanted as speakers. A very large church on one occasion invited Add to preach in both the morning and evening services in the absence of the regular minister. Several thousand people attended the morning service, but just before the assistant minister led Add out to the platform for the evening service he whispered to him, "Now, Dr. Leitch, there won't be nearly as many people here tonight as there were this morning. I hope you won't feel bad. Sometimes we've had really *good* speakers, and they don't show up for them either."

On another occasion a "name brand" speaker had been invited and widely advertised in Pittsburgh, but a few days before the scheduled appearance he became ill. Add was asked to substitute. The man who introduced him faced the house packed with those who had come to hear the Big Name and apologized, explaining that they had tried several other substitutes who could not accept—"so, in our desperation, we turned to Dr. Leitch." Add's opening remark was, "I hope you realize what a favor it is I'm doing you. If I had refused

117

just imagine what the *next* man down the list would have been like!"

Once at a club luncheon of several hundred people Add was seated at the head table between the president of the organization and the treasurer, who argued across him during the meal about what they would pay the speaker who was, of course, Add himself. At last Add decided to help them out and suggested that since he had noticed that nearly everyone there had had a cocktail before lunch, perhaps he could just settle for the price of a cocktail per head. The two officers blanched, the treasurer stuttering that after all it was a charity organization and twenty-five dollars was really all they could manage. "Never mind," said Add, "I'm a charity organization myself. Just get me home."

A few years ago I arrived at a church where I was to give a talk for a ladies' luncheon. As happens with somewhat dismaying frequency, no one seemed to be expecting me and I stood for a long time in the foyer while very busy women rushed by with casseroles and centerpieces. At length a lady greeted me in a friendly but not an official way. I introduced myself and saw at once that the name meant nothing. I asked if she knew Mrs. Jones, the lady with whom I had corresponded. Yes, she thought probably Mrs. Jones was in the kitchen. She would find her. Off she went and returned after some minutes with a lady, both of them peering curiously at me as they crossed a large room. The first lady said nothing when they reached me, so I introduced myself again to the second lady who looked baffled. "Oh, my goodness!" she exclaimed, as she recovered herself. "You certainly look a lot older than your pictures!" (This might be a lesson to all speakers to make sure the photo they send out is a current one, but in my case it was. Either the photographer had succeeded in showing me in a flattering light, or the lady had seen only earlier pictures.)

When a speaker receives more invitations than he can accept, a very small thing may make the difference between yes and no. I am influenced by the tone of a letter. If it seems I am being offered a platform, or that the writer is saying, "we might be able to work you into our program," I am not always galvanized into acceptance. If somebody I never heard of telephones and starts right in with my first name I am inclined to back off a little.

I usually want to say yes when I receive a straightforward, simple letter telling me who wants me, where, when, what the occasion is, what I am to talk about, and for how long. I appreciate it when money is candidly mentioned in the first communication. The choice is then mine, not the inviter's, as to whether this is to be a charity operation or not. For many years it was customary for churches to "give" speakers "whatever the Lord laid on their hearts," and sometimes it looked as though the Lord were not aware of the price of gasoline. The speaker is in a better position to make his decision if he knows in advance what to expect. I have done many "benefits" and am sometimes glad to do them, but they have not always been voluntary.

It is very hard to visualize an audience and an atmosphere. I am always grateful if in subsequent letters I am given some idea of the total program into which I am supposed to fit. It makes a difference to a speaker if the audience will be sitting in church pews or folding chairs, or squatting on the floor in front of a lodge fire, whether they will be eager note-takers and tape-recorders, or coffee drinkers and needlepointers, whether the speaker is to sit on a sofa or at a table, or to stand, with or without a lectern and microphone.

It is helpful to know where the people are with regard to the subject to be treated, and whether there will be books for sale which some of them will already have read or which they will be likely to buy.

When I get where I am going it is reassuring to be met by somebody who knows what's happening, who will take me to the motel if it is an overnight engagement, inform me as to when and where I am to eat, when he will pick me up for the meeting, and then *leave me alone* long enough to collect my wits. Even when no overnight accommodations are necessary, it is a great help to have some place to be quiet for a little while, especially if it is an all-day affair with several appearances and people wanting to get at the speaker in every available minute in between. I have sometimes had to escape to a parked car outside a church in order to sort things out between meetings.

Occasionally there is a business meeting before the speaker comes on. I am sure there will be special rewards in heaven for those who have somehow seen to it that the speaker need not sit through the financial reports, the debates about next spring's banquet, and all the committee reports from the preceding six months before he makes his speech.

Introductions can be painful. Sometimes the person responsible for introducing the speaker has been badly informed, or gives far more information than the audience cares to hear. Sometimes he doesn't say enough. Once my introduction, in its entirety, was, "Our speaker this evening is Mrs. Leitch." This leaves the speaker in the uncomfortable position of feeling that he must defend his right to address this gathering, answering the "Who are you?" and "What are you doing here?" that the audience has a right to ask.

Sometimes there is a question period following the lecture. I am hugely relieved if somebody else takes charge of this, sorts out the questions, steers them to the point and winds things up within a reasonable time.

And then there is the cake and coffee. As a speaker, I know that I have been a miserable offender in every possible way, not the least of which has been my unwillingness to stand in line for the homemade goodies that everybody else has been looking forward to all evening. I'm grateful when somebody just comes along and hands me a cup of tea or whatever.

As I think of the past ten years I remember the priceless opportunities that have been mine—to meet so many different kinds of people, so many varieties of Christians, so kind, so eager, so open and humble and loving and encouraging, people who have helped me more than I could possibly have helped them. Some of the greatest people I know (my husband, for example) I have met because somebody invited me to speak. So the last thing I would like to say about all this (and I hope it hasn't sounded picky) is thanks. Thanks for wanting me—it's wonderful to be wanted—thanks for listening, thanks for being my friends.

* * *

Question-and-answer, too, is a vanishing art. We are so drowned and smothered and deafened by panels, dialogues, rap sessions, discussions, talk shows and other such exercises in the pooling of ignorance that, far from developing the art of asking questions and giving answers, we have very nearly lost it altogether. The time allotted for a program must, it seems, be filled—it doesn't much matter with what.

When is the last time you heard a clear, short question asked and a straight answer given? My heart sinks when it is announced that, following the lecture, there will be time for discussion. People put up their hands, but it turns out that it is not information they are after at all. They want the floor. They go on and on.

I was one of a panel of experts (i.e., married women) discussing the subject of marriage in a college

121

women's dormitory a few weeks ago. Afterward there were lots of questions. But it was hard to figure out just what the questions were. Here is one of them (*verbatim*—I did not make this up. It was taped and then transcribed):

"Um—like—um—I have a couple questions. Do you think—like—that—uh—do you think a woman could have a call just to be—like—a wife, but not—like—not *just* to be a wife—like, say, you know—if you're gonna be personal—like—my own engagement—like—I have a gift of—you know—a talent in music, you know—like—I mean, I know you're not saying—like—you know, especially in that case, I mean, you're saying more like—you have—like—I think our greatest thing in common probably is—um—is that—you know—is the dedication to serve God—you know—in the desire to, to follow—you know—to do his leading and—like—neither of us, you know, and especially in this kind of life you don't have a blueprint of what you—what he's gonna be doing necessarily, you know—and I'm just kinda concerned because like—you know—I've even thought about that cause I've kinda had a conflict—you know—growing up that way—you know—I'm talented musically—you know—so therefore I should probably look for somebody that's talented musically but he—he likes it—you know—I mean, he doesn't understand it totally but I'm sure we could live happily together with it, you know, but I don't expect him to have a—you know—yearning to go to all the Beethoven concerts or anything—you know—but I mean—I've heard of very happy marriages where—you know—there's quite different—you know—interests—you know—there."

(I apologize for not knowing the rules of punctuation for this kind of English.) Nobody on the panel knew what the girl was asking. She was confused—that came through loud and clear, but she might have seen through some of the fog simply by making the effort to clarify and shorten her question.

Sometimes I have been tempted to tell the audience that only questions of twenty-five words or less will be entertained. But I don't want to put people off any more than I can help.

William Strunk, Jr., in his wonderful little book *The Elements of Style,* gives this advice: "To air one's views at an improper time may be in bad taste. If you have received a letter inviting you to speak at the dedication of a new cat hospital, and you hate cats, your reply, declining the invitation, does not necessarily have to cover the full range of your emotions. You must make it clear that you will not attend, but you do not have to let fly at cats. . . . Bear in mind that your opinion of cats was not sought, only your services as a speaker. Try to keep things straight."

Americans dearly love to be polled for opinion. They feel that they ought to have opinions, to "hold views," on everything, and polls give them a chance to let fly. It is interesting to note how small a percentage of those polled admit to having "No opinion."

If the answer is Yes, say Yes. If it's No, say No. (The Bible will back me up here.) If it's I don't know, say that—if you possibly can. My daughter had a classmate in the seventh grade who, when asked a question by the teacher, never raised his chin off his hand, but looking into space said glumly, "I don't know." To a second question he replied, in the same laconic tone, "I don't know that either." I couldn't help wanting to know which boy that was. I liked him. It was discouraging for the teacher, I'm sure, that he didn't know, but it was not nearly so discouraging to hear him say so in three words as it would have been to hear three hundred words which came to the same thing. Every day in the mass media we have to listen to palaver, twaddle, and balderdash which, when interpreted, means "I don't know."

Some people are constitutionally incapable of admitting they don't know. "Well, let's just say I don't know the answer to that one," a woman once said to me.

Great people, however, can often disarm us completely with a candid acknowledgment such as Samuel Johnson's when asked by an indignant woman what ever made him define *pastern* as he did in his lexicon. "Ignorance, Madam, pure ignorance!"

The Quichua Indians of Ecuador have a way of dropping the corners of their mouths, thrusting out their chins and gazing off across the treetops, saying "Hmm hmm?" which is supposed to convey the impression that the matter is a mysterious one which they are in on but which would really be beyond you. At other times they come up with ineluctable answers like the one a missionary got when he wanted to know the name of a tree with yellow flowers on it. The Indian studied the tree for a little while, shading his eyes with his hand, and then said earnestly, "Well, I'll tell you, Senor Eduardo. That tree over there, the one you point to, the tree with the yellow flowers on it—that tree, Senor Eduardo, we call The Yellow Flower Tree."

The late W. H. Auden once appeared on a television interview and it was delicious to see his interviewers thrown completely off balance by the clarity and the brevity of his answers. They had their questions carefully worked out and the timing approximated, but long before the show was over they were casting about for new questions. When they asked if he thought of poetry as a means of self-expression, he said, "No, not at all. You write a poem because you have seen something which seems worth sharing with others. The ideal reaction from the reader is, 'I knew that all along, but I never realized it.' " He could, I am sure, have lectured for an hour on that one subject, but he didn't. He had a sense of occasion.

"You will be living in Oxford, England, Mr. Auden. Do you expect to be teaching there?"

"No."

"You won't be teaching." (Pause) "Well, Mr. Auden, as you move into the more—shall we say—mellow years, would you say that you have any unfulfilled ambitions?"

"No."

One of my unfulfilled ambitions was to hear a simple answer on a TV talk show. Thank you, Mr. Auden.

Two Ladies' Meetings

FOR REASONS THAT are not always entirely clear, it is generally assumed that people who write should also speak. This has its pleasures and privileges as well as its drawbacks, and sometimes a speaking invitation which I have accepted with reluctance has led me into unexpected delights.

I came back from the beautiful Shenandoah Valley of Virginia sometime ago with a ceramic pitcher, a record, a big recipe book and a small history book in my suitcase. These were gifts from individuals who belong to an amazing group of people called Mennonites. The pitcher came from a lady who had made it herself, glazed it and painted a delicate design of pine boughs on it. There are pretty pitchers, and there are useful ones—this one is both for it pours perfectly.

The record is a collection of unaccompanied songs sung by nine hundred college students. I would not have believed that students could or would sing without a guitar; but these are students at Eastern Mennonite College in Harrisonburg, Virginia, and they come from generations of people who, from religious conviction, excluded instrumental accompaniment in their churches and, as a result, know how to sing four parts, in perfect time, and with great depth and quality.

The recipe book is the *Mennonite Community Cookbook* by Mary Emma Showalter, who was my hostess. It has everything in it from shoofly pie and sour cherry soup to "Dutch goose," which is roasted pig's stomach, and the menu for 175 barn raisers, found written by hand in the author's great-grandmother's notebook. Here it is:*

115 lemon pies
500 fat cakes (doughnuts)
15 large cakes
3 gallons applesauce
3 gallons rice pudding
3 gallons cornstarch pudding
16 chickens
3 hams
50 pounds roast beef
300 light rolls
16 loaves bread
Red beet pickle and pickled eggs
Cucumber pickle
6 pounds dried stewed prunes
1 large crock raisins
5 gallon stone jar white potatoes
5 gallon stone jar sweet potatoes

The ceramics, the singing, the good cooking, all come out of this remarkable group. Who are these Mennonites anyway? I was glad that the fourth gift was a history book called *Mennonites and Their Heritage,* by Harold S. Bender and C. Henry Smith, which tells of the origin of the movement in the sixteenth century in Zurich. A baker, a tailor, a cooper, a bookseller, a goldsmith and a young university student named Conrad Grebel were in the group which had come together with a deep conviction that the existing church was not following the pattern of the New Testament. Others desiring to obey the commands of Scripture as literally

* From *Mennonite Community Cookbook* by Mary Emma Showalter. Copyright © 1950, 1957 by Mary Emma Showalter. Herald Press, Scottdale, Pa. 15683. Used by permission.

as possible joined them; and the movement spread over Europe, arousing suspicion and then hatred. Felix Manz, one of Grebel's colleagues, was executed by drowning in 1527. George Blaurock was burned at the stake. Michael Sattler, formerly the prior of a Black Forest monastery, was tortured and then burned. Menno Simons, a priest from Holland, embraced the principles of the Swiss "Brethren," and it is from him that the modern denomination derives its name.

There are over four hundred thousand Mennonites in the world today, more than half of them in the United States, the rest in Europe, Asia, Africa, and South America. I keep meeting them in unexpected places and hearing things about them; and they are always busy, always doing things for other people without advertising; but when I speak of them to other brands of Christians there is always some slight surprise. Not that people haven't heard of them. I discovered that it's a little like being from New Hampshire, which people often confuse with Vermont. "You're from Vermont? Oh—New Hampshire. Well . . ."

Mennonites? Yes—they're those people with the black hats and the buggies. Oh, those are the Amish. You mean there are other kinds? In Ontario? Kansas? Virginia? I thought they were all in Pennsylvania, along the turnpike. The ones with the signs (what do you call them?) on their barns.

No, I tell them. There's much more to it. The meeting I attended in Virginia, for example, was in a country church on a Thursday morning. Hundreds of women flocked in. They drove cars, not carriages, and they all wore modern dresses. None wore makeup. They were an extraordinarily attentive and intelligent audience, and they proved to be great readers and book buyers and very friendly.

But one part of that meeting impressed me profoundly. Mimeographed sheets had been given out ahead of time on which 119 separate missionary needs were listed. The needs ranged from green-stamp books to projectors, clothing, medical supplies and magazine subscriptions. A lady stood up and asked for a show of hands of those who had selected a first choice—a need from the list which they were willing to supply. Up went fifty or more hands. A board up front contained cards with numbers from one to 119.

As each of the numbers was called out, another lady removed the cards. Then the second choice was asked for. Up went more hands. Only a few dozen cards were left on the board at the end of that meeting, and before the next meeting the board was empty—119 different needs met in a matter of an hour! Besides this, pledges were received amounting to several thousand dollars, two very large offerings were taken, and volunteers were called for to mend (by this time my head was spinning) tons of clothing donated for the West Virginia flood victims.

And this goes on all the time. Not that the Mennonites are the only people working for the good of others, but when I see it happen I want to know why. So much done by so few for so many, and so constantly and consistently—why?

The founders, Grebel, Simons and their associates, insisted upon "the practice of the presence of Christ *in action.*" The principle of full brotherhood and stewardship of the gifts of God found its expression in visible and practical ways, such as the sharing of material possessions. The grace of giving has been *taught,* line upon line and precept upon precept. It is learned as one of the things a Christian *does.* He knows the meaning of sacrifice, of putting himself out for the sake of others.

Then, not long ago I attended a lecture at a prestigious divinity school. It was a lovely spring day and the audience was made up of ladies (mostly the wives of theological professors) and they enjoyed coming out to hear a nice man on a nice subject, "The Search for a New Theory of Mission." I took notes but couldn't quite tell whether he had found anything to suggest. During the question period which followed, it became embarrassingly clear that few of them had the faintest idea what missionary work was about.

"I never could see this business of going out and telling the whole world that your religion is better than theirs," one lady said, and heads nodded in agreement.

"Do-gooders," "world-savers," the "rhetoric of conquest"—"who buys that sort of thing in this day and age?" But the confusion was more compounded when the lady went on to say that on the other hand, missionaries actually have *schools*. She had seen them in Africa. They *teach* African children! And, said another, there are some missionaries in Pakistan who have a hospital in which they treat *Pakistanis*. So really, you see, they can't be all bad. No, it was generally agreed, there must be something to be said for them.

Having said it, however, let no one inquire too closely into what theory lies behind that action. The ladies were here to discuss a new theory.

My mind went back to that incredibly productive hour with the Mennonites in Virginia, to the theory that produced that kind of action, the same theory that Sattler and Blaurock were willing to be buried alive for.

There is no formula for success comparable to Christ's own: "Except a corn of wheat fall into the ground and die, it abideth alone. But if it die, it bringeth forth much fruit."

III

RISK AND SERVICE

Adequate Coverage

CIVILIZATION, someone said, is life arranged so that it doesn't have to be experienced. I like that, because I am always thinking about the contrasts between us privileged and developed peoples and others. We spend nearly all of our time protecting ourselves from one thing or another. The symbol of an insurance company is an umbrella, a relatively simple, protective device which has been used in some form for a good many centuries. In the jungle west of the Andes, where the Colorado Indians live, giant elephant-ear plants grow. The leaves make wonderful raincoats. They are heart shaped and often four or five feet long. You fold the two rounded tabs over your shoulders with your neck in the slot, hold onto the stem, and the long point reaches down over your back almost to your heels. An umbrella, of course, keeps your head but not much else dry. The elephant ear keeps all but your head dry. So when it comes right down to it, you wouldn't call either "adequate coverage." But we do the best we can.

In this country we hardly know what it is to experience that which for most people in most places has been an inescapable fact of life: weather. We have waterproofing and insulation and paving and Thermopane. We go from a humidified or a dehumidified and air-conditioned or heated house to a heated or air-conditioned car. We travel anywhere we want to go on roads that are made for all weathers. Very few of our decisions depend solely on the weather. We need not worry that food will or will not be on our tables six months from now according to what the weather does to our crop, because we don't have crops. Somebody else has them, and if his don't grow somebody's will.

We are protected from illness by immunizations and prophylactics of all sorts, or at least from its worst effects by medicines and pain killers. We are freed from insects inside by screens and outside by repellents and insecticides. We are protected from all kinds of bother: We have paper towels, paper handkerchiefs, Handi-Wipes, disposable dishes, permanent-press fabrics, prepared foods, ready-mixed drinks, spray cans of a thousand liquids which, with only a little bother, we could apply otherwise. We try to protect ourselves from weeds we don't want with weed killers, from smells we don't want with deodorizers, from fat we don't want (which is the result of food we do want) with girdles, Exercycles, diet pills, from aging with Geritol, face-lifting, hair dyes and wigs. We shield ourselves from tensions with tranquilizers, and from people—all kinds of people we don't want around—with burglar alarms, locks, fences and with secretaries and club memberships and restricted residential areas and who knows how many little private ways of faking and hiding and dissimulating.

We have insurance. We pay for coverage for accidents to ourselves and to our property (it's a good idea to read the small print to be sure about falling aircraft, barratry, or acts of God), but I've noticed that the pictures in the ads show a man with a broken leg or a cheerful convalescent in a hospital receiving his insurance check. They usually stick to scenes like that. They don't show coffins.

We have done well. We are civilized. There isn't much of life that we have to experience if we don't want to and we can choose what we do want on the TV dial without any risks. Our lives are secure in ways that simpler people would find unimaginable. Not much weather, not many snakes or falling trees or vampires worry us, not often does an epidemic affect our population, nor seldom do we even get a thorn in our foot. Indeed, few of us have been cursed by a witchdoctor or met up with a demon. But then we've got worries the uncivilized have never thought of: where to find a plumber who'll come this week instead of next, what to do for a son hooked on dope or a pregnant teen-age daughter, or questions such as: Will pollution kill us all? What about nuclear fall-out?

And we feel cornered. We know that we have done badly. While we've managed to exempt ourselves quite neatly from a lot that the rest of the world has had to put up with, we've also placed ourselves into frightful things. Only recently I was given an article written back in 1964, "National Security and the Nuclear-Test Ban," by Jerome B. Wiesner and Herbert F. York, about "the hopelessness of the task of defense."

The authors explain how the Department of Defense has tried to develop systems adequate for defense against all known weapons, but the degree of uncertainty in predicting the number and kind of weapons that might be available to prospective attackers increases steadily. "Both sides in the arms race are confronted by the dilemma of steadily increasing military power and steadily decreasing national security. It is our considered professional judgment that this dilemma has no technical solution. . . . The clearly predictable course of the arms race is a steady open spiral downward into oblivion."

You read that and you draw your breath in slowly and realize that against the monstrous blast your insurance and other protection are about as useful as an umbrella. There's no coverage.

Yesterday I wrote a letter to a friend whose husband

had just been killed. A stickler all his life for seat belts and stop signs, he was thrown from his car when he didn't see a sign and was struck by another car. As I wrote the letter I pictured Margie, climbing out of the upside-down car, wondering why Dick didn't answer her children's calls, finding him then by the roadside and realizing all of a sudden that she was a widow, her children were fatherless and she would have to learn now to say "I" instead of "we," because Dick wouldn't be there anymore.

Our civilization protects us from life all right in many ways. But it hasn't done much about death except to postpone it for some and to create new ways to die. What kind of coverage do we have, anyway? What do you say in the letter to your friend?

Well, there is something. And it is everything. For the one who has to go on living, these words: "I am sure that neither death, nor life, nor angels, nor principalities, nor things present nor things to come, nor powers, nor height, nor depth, nor anything else in all creation, will be able to separate us from the love of God in Christ Jesus our Lord."

And for the one who has died, these words: "The trumpet will sound, and the dead will be raised imperishable, and we shall be changed. For this perishable nature must put on the imperishable, and this mortal nature must put on immortality."

For me, there is nowhere else where such a thing as coverage exists. But here it is, and it is not merely adequate. It is total.

* * *

Yet the risks people are prepared to take these days are certainly a different set from what they used to be. I have been reading what Dickens and Kipling said about travel in their times. The reason I have been reading Dickens and Kipling just now when I am also trying to catch up with Solzhenitsyn and C.S. Lewis (I never catch up with Lewis—I have to start over as soon as I've finished one of his books because while I am always completely convinced by his argument I find I can't reproduce it for somebody else so I have to go back) is that a friend asked me to take care of some books she had just inherited from a rich aunt.

But it was risks I started out to write about. Dickens describes a journey into the Scottish Highlands. "When we got safely to the opposite bank, there came riding up a wild highlander, his great plaid streaming in the wind, screeching in Gaelic to the post-boy on the opposite bank, making the most frantic gestures . . . The boy, horses and carriage were plunging in the water, which left only the horses' heads and boy's body visible . . . The man was perfectly frantic with pantomime . . . The carriage went round and round like a great stone, the boy was pale as death, the horses were struggling and splashing and snorting like sea animals, and we were all roaring to the driver to throw himself off and let them and the coach go to the devil, when suddenly it all came right (having got into shallow water) and, all tumbling and dripping and jogging from side to side, they climbed up to the dry land."

Kipling, in a speech made sixty years ago to the Royal Geographic Society, looks forward to the possibilities of air travel: "Presently—very presently—we shall come back and convert two hundred miles across any part of the Earth into its standardized time equivalent, precisely as we convert five miles with infantry in column, ten with cavalry on the march, twelve in a Cape cart [which I found is a strong, two-wheeled carriage used in South Africa], or fifty in a car—that is to say, into two hours. And whether there be one desert or a dozen mountain ranges in that two hundred miles will not affect our timetable by five minutes."

137

Traveling nowadays means what it has always meant: facing risks. Take air travel, for example. There is, of course, the total risk—a crash—but most of us, when it comes to actually getting on a plane, are not preoccupied with that possibility. We are much more conscious of the sort of risk that calls forth no very high courage. Weather, topography, sources of food and water along the way hardly concern us at all. We expect the aircraft itself, the radar, the pilots, the mechanics, the caterers and the stewardesses to do their jobs and we forget about them from the start. We worry instead about whether we will get stuck in the middle seat between two (perhaps fat) people who use both arms of their seats, whether we'll have leg room after we've stuffed our bag underneath the seat in front of us, and whether a talkative seatmate will ruin our plans to get some serious reading done on a coast-to-coast flight.

There is a white paper bag in the seat-pocket reminding us of another risk, "motion discomfort," which has superseded what sounds like a worse one, airsickness. The stewardess's voice comes over the intercom at takeoff, while another stewardess goes through a pantomime, telling us where to find the emergency exits and what to do in "the extremely unlikely event of a change in cabin pressure," and we pay no attention.

The apostle Paul was shipwrecked three times. He had to spend twenty-four hours in the open sea. He wrote to the Corinthians: "In my travels I have been in constant danger from rivers and floods, from bandits, from my own countrymen and from pagans. I have faced danger in city streets, danger in the desert, danger on the high seas, danger among false Christians. I have known exhaustion, pain, long vigils, hunger and thirst, doing without meals, cold and lack of clothing."

Well, Paul, once in a trans-oceanic flight in something called a jumbo jet my daughter watched a movie for a whole hour before she realized that the soundtrack she had plugged into her ears was for another movie. (What do I mean by "flight?" "Movie?" "Soundtrack?" Never mind. They're all of them hazards you never had to cope with.) On top of that, the reading lights didn't work, there was no soap in the lavatories, no pillows or blankets on board although the air-conditioning was functioning only too well, and they served dinner at eleven o'clock at night and breakfast at one in the morning.

We take risks, all right. But what acquaintance have we with the physical hardships which used to be the testing ground for a man's character and stamina? We know nothing of the necessity of covering ground with our own two feet for days or weeks or months at a time, every step of which must be retraced on those same two feet if we're ever to get back to civilization again. We haven't felt the panic of isolation beyond help. When a book like *Alive: The Story of the Andes Survivors* appears, it becomes a best seller for we recognize then the hermetic seal of our civilization.

An ancient longing for danger, for challenge and for sacrifice stirs in us—us who have insulated ourselves from weather by heating and air-conditioning and waterproofing and Thermopane; from bugs, germs, pests and odors by screening, repellents, insecticides, weed-killers, disinfectants and deodorizers; from poverty by insurance, Medicare and Social Security; from theft by banks, locks, Mace and burglar alarms; from having to watch others suffer by putting them where somebody else will do the watching and from guilt by calling any old immorality a "new morality," or by joining a group that encourages everybody to do whatever feels good.

We don't risk involvement if we can help it. We try not to turn around if anybody screams. Responsibility for others we'd rather delegate to institutions, including the government, which are supposed to make it their business to handle it.

I saw a man on television just a few days after Mr. Ford became President telling us that what America needs is a little more honesty. Because of technology, the man said, people have to be more dependent on each other than they used to be (Oh?) and therefore we need more honesty (Oh). Probably, he allowed, our standards have never been quite what they ought to be and it's time to hike them up a notch or two.

How do we go about this? Take a deep breath and—all together now—start being honest? Ah, the man had a plan. I waited, tense and eager, to hear what it might be. Popularization was what he proposed. Make honesty the In Thing. If everybody's doing it, it will be easy. In fact, the bright-eyed man told us, it would take the risk out of it.

Funny, I always thought righteousness was supposed to be risky. I was taught it wasn't easy, and I found it hard when I tried it. It's never likely to be either easy or popular.

"But I'm not asking for a change in human nature or anything," the man on the TV insisted; "only a change in attitude." And the round-eyed artlessness with which the remark was made and with which it was received by the TV "host" was breathtaking.

I'm for civilization. I'm all for certain kinds of progress and I accept quite gladly most of today's means of avoiding the risks that Dickens and Kipling and all of mankind before them had to run, but to imagine that we shall whip off the dishonesty that is characteristic of fallen human nature everywhere as painlessly as we whip off one garment and put on another, to imagine that by simply taking a different view we shall come up with a no-risk brand of honesty, is a piece of self-deception and fatuity to make the mind reel.

Plato, three hundred years before Christ, predicted that if ever the truly good man were to appear, the man who would tell the truth, he would have his eyes gouged out and in the end be crucified.

That risk was once taken, in its fullest measure. The man appeared. He told the world the truth about itself and even made the proposterous claim "I am the Truth." As Plato foresaw, that man was crucified.

He calls us still to follow him, and the conditions are the same: "Let a man deny himself and take up his cross."

Is There a Hero in the House?

THE *New Yorker* carried a cartoon once which showed a pickup truck with the words *Haarlem Dike Emergency Repair Service* lettered on the door. In the back of the truck were six or eight small Dutch boys.

An exceptionally good joke, I thought. And it struck not only my funnybone but something deeper. All that business about the town of Haarlem being saved from destruction by the sacrifice of a boy in wooden shoes had thrilled me as a child. He had done the one thing possible when he put his finger in the leak. He suffered. I suffered with him as he stood through long hours, finger aching, then arm, back, and whole body racked and tortured. But he stood. He was "Hans, the Hero of Haarlem."

Does anyone do things like that anymore? Does anyone notice if they do? But this cartoon—can heroism be organized, commercialized, multiplied? If so, there isn't much thrill left in it. It's just a good joke.

Yet we still need heroes, and we need them desperately. I suppose it is partly because we are conscious of failure and ordinariness in ourselves, and we need to be cheered on by the sight of someone who is successful or extraordinary in one way or another. The classic hero of the past was a person of noble character, of fortitude in suffering, of unusual enterprise in danger. There came a time when the thing to do was to debunk all heroes, to smile tolerantly or even to sneer at what looked like greatness, and to attempt as loudly as possible to advertise the weaknesses of leaders. (Was it a relief to find that there was no need after all to praise anybody?) More recently the hero often hailed by the crowd is a non-hero, a man devoid of any quality of greatness. He is vapid and faceless and certainly not tragic, but only pathetic. Those who follow such a hero are pathetic, too, for he is unable to take them anywhere.

It is a bad thing to make something out of nothing. If there are no longer any real heroes, if the world has no chance for a glimpse of greatness, we shall in our bankruptcy have to make something out of nothing. Non-heroes, presumably, are better than no heroes at all. We have given up the outdated kind, the shining visions of knights in armor or towering kings who ruled in righteousness. We have new supermen: a Batman or a James Bond, whom we can get away with worshiping openly as long as we tell ourselves he's "high camp," or just a put-on. Quite without our realizing it, however, we have come to lump real heroes with Batman and 007. Heroism is nothing more than a put-on. To be *honest* nowadays is to recognize that one man is as bad and as laughable as the next, and the more thoroughly we can demonstrate his rottenness and his absurdity the more cheered we shall be as we contemplate our own.

We are all of us at times bad and laughable, but there are still also among us now and then truth, greatness, even holiness. The merest hint of true holiness we are quick to suspect as counterfeit, and we condemn what we like to call a "holier than thou" attitude. But years ago a teacher pointed out that the person I was condemning was in fact holier than I—and it certainly didn't take much.

George Eliot, in her incomparable novel *Middlemarch,* tells of a certain vicar who "had escaped being a Pharisee, but he had not escaped that low estimate of possibilities which we rather hastily arrive at as an inference from our own failure."

Because we ourselves bump along the low road, accommodating ourselves, compromising, making outrageously generous allowances for ourselves alone (such as saying, "That's the way I am, I have to do my thing," or calling old-fashioned, banal sins "frustrations" or "hang-ups") we begin to find it less and less possible to believe that there really are some who travel a higher road and that they have reached it perhaps by genuine courage, sacrifice, or the kind of self-giving love that the Bible tells us about.

It is a bad thing to make something out of nothing, to make a hero out of a discouragingly common sort of person, or worse, out of one who has distinguished himself by degradation alone. Eliot's vicar did an equally bad thing. He made nothing out of something. Both errors come from failure to value things as they truly are. We end up magnifying the trivial and minimizing the great.

I have written a book or two which have been taken by some of my readers as attempts to make nothing out of something, to debunk. A mere description of one event in one missionary's life (a conference on "the field") was read not as a description at all but as an attack on the whole scheme of modern missions, and even on the validity of Christ's great commission. "Are you determined," asked some wrathful readers, "to demolish the work of the Lord?" No, I had tried to recreate a scene. This is how it looked there, this is the way these particular missionaries spoke and acted. I had not tried to make it more or less that it was. "Are there no good missionaries?" questioned others. This question had me utterly baffled. A simple count of the characters in my book would have shown more goodies than baddies, or I don't know a goodie when I see one.

Later I wrote the true story of what happened in the life of a missionary who was nearly a hero by reputation during the latter part of his life, and whose death has, as often happens, made him a full hero to many. But some readers were convinced I had tried to make him a nothing; that I had searched meticulously for the negative aspects of his experience and personality in order to expose gleefully the feet of clay.

My model for this and an earlier biography had been the Bible. Men are shown there for what they are: far less than perfect, but far more than nothing. And a few readers, to my immense encouragement, wrote that they had been able to identify with Kenneth Strachan, my biography, principally because they had found him a man of "like passions" with themselves, a flawed human being, but one who had, in spite of his sins, sought the will of God, David, clearly shown to be both an adulterer and a murderer in the Bible, was yet a man whose heart was "perfect toward God."

An evangelical magazine carried a discussion not long ago on the missionary as hero. To say with a shrug, "Oh, this missionary hero bit . . ." implies that it's *all* nonsense. But to ask, "Are missionaries really heroes?" is beside the point. Some missionaries (and some knights, some sailors, some plumbers and housewives) are heroes, whether we like it or not. One of the writers in the magazines said, "The truth comes not through sentimental biographies peppered with anecdotes, but through facts." He was mixed up. The truth may indeed *come through* a sentimental biography peppered with anecdotes, for anecdotes, after all, may be facts, and very interesting ones, too. I for one would like it a lot better without the sentimentality. This cuts off some of the light. But an anecdote may well carry the truth of a man's life, as Jesus' parables showed heavenly truth, and may stun us into the awareness that we are looking at a great person: the man who did

145

this, the woman who endured that. The abolition of heroes is easier said than done, for the world still contains them. Far be it from me to wish to debunk them. Just as far be it to wish to make a man look larger than life (which is what we mean when we speak artistically of "heroic" proportion). My job as a biographer was to try as hard as I could to show the man in life size, not smaller, not greater. This is impossible, for my own judgment is imperfect. Yet I try for it.

Let me remember his frailties, not to show him up as a mere put-on, but only so that I may not excuse myself from achieving what he achieved. If I regard him as invulnerable and blameless I shall take refuge in my own weakness and never aim at strength. Let me study his glory (whatever in him was really admirable) as a continual proof that men who were weak became strong, men who suffered passions and temptations that I suffer nevertheless rose above them. Even if they rose only for a moment, let me grasp the truth of that moment.

* * *

Recently I read in the paper that a woman was planning to sail the Atlantic alone. Good idea, I thought. If you like to sail, it would certainly be fun to sail across a whole ocean, and it might be interesting to sail it alone. I can easily sympathize with people's wanting to tackle a tough job, even if it's unnecessary, if it strikes them as a good adventure. (Men and women used to have real adventures in the ordinary and necessary course of their lives, but it doesn't seem to happen that way much anymore. We've inoculated and insulated and insured and protected ourselves against most kinds of adventure, so that we now have to go out looking for them.) The part in the news story that made me say, "Oh dear," was the announcement that the lone sailor was going to tape record her emotions throughout the voyage. No, I thought, I don't want to hear about it. If the lady was going because she liked to sail, she might give us a good story when she got back, but if she was in search of an "experience" which would elicit certain emotions she was hoping to have, I doubt that the complete transcription would be something very many of us would like to hear.

Why is it, I wonder, that the question, How do you feel about this? has taken on such huge significance today? It is not a question concerning the thing done, nor the purpose in doing it. People seem to have lost their objectives, to have forgotten what they are trying to do.

In the movie *Patton* the general encounters a soldier lying on the floor.

"What the ——— are you doing?" he roars.

Leaping to his feet and saluting, the soldier stammers, "I'm just trying to get some sleep, Sir."

"Well, get the ——— back down on the floor, then," says Patton. "You're the only ——— ——— around here that knows what he's trying to do."

The question, "How do you feel?" strikes me as aimless. Suppose a clear answer can be given; then where are we? What do we know, in most cases, that is worth knowing?

The city of Boston had a Cleanup Day a few weeks ago when thousands turned out on the Common with brooms, rakes and plastic trash bags. A TV interviewer nabbed a teen-age girl to ask the big question.

"I think it's beautiful," the girl answered. "I mean, you know it's like fun, a lot of people getting together and all."

"How does your mother feel about it?"

She shifted her gum to work the other side of her mouth.

"My mother?"

"Yeah."

"Oh well," she said, "you know, she wished I'd, like, clean up my own room before I started on Boston Common. But, I mean, that's a typical mother reaction."

The girl laughed and went on sweeping and chewing.

Our sudden self-conscious effort in this technological age to treat people as people has made us act as though the be-all and end-all of life lies inside us, in our psyche, and as though the highest reason—often the only reason—for doing or not doing a thing is a feeling. I saw a poster put up by the youth group in a church which said, "If it feels good, do it."

For a few years I worked on some Indian languages in South America. I found in each of them a tremendous wealth of vigorous verbs and onomatopoeic words, but very few terms which describe emotion. How they felt about things was best discerned by what they did, not by what they said. I shared the emotions of the hunt not by the hunter's describing for me how he really felt during the chase, but by his telling me in detail where he was, where the animal was, what he saw, what he heard—the specific noises of the spear slicing through the air, the thunk when it sank into the flesh of the prey, the grunt or bleat or scream of agony as the animal was impaled, and the sound of the fall to the ground. The hunter was after food, not an emotional experience, but in this necessary work he found a huge pleasure which he managed also to give me just by the telling of the story. He experienced emotions which a man who hunted for the sake of the thrill would probably miss altogether.

It wasn't all thrills, of course. The Indian endured some terrific hardships, but he hadn't many words for those either. Weather was what I would call bad for hiking in the rain forest most of the time. But it was not talked about. The heavy burdens the Indians carried on their backs, the deep mud they ploughed through, the steep hills climbed and ravines descended, the heat and gnats and thorns were matters of course. They endured these without comment most of the time, doing what they had to do regardless of the difficulties, regardless of their feelings. They were far from unfeeling—I am convinced of this—though a superficial acquaintance with them might give the impression that they felt nothing. It wasn't that nothing mattered. They knew exactly what they were doing. Their aims were perfectly clear and they were what mattered. Feelings were simply not given much attention.

This is one of the things that made these people interesting. The trouble with hearing how everybody feels about everything is that after awhile hardly any of it is interesting. No wonder talk shows are almost all the same. No wonder kids' faces are so expressionless. Everybody is looking inside. There aren't any horizons.

We hear a lot about the need for sharing. I am all for sharing what I have that others want, but too often the word means loading what we can't stand—our disappointments, hostilities, frustrations, burdens of all kinds—onto other people's shoulders. We ought to be willing, the Bible tells us, to bear one another's burdens, but each man is told also to bear his own. It is a big thing we ask when we lay them on somebody else, a thing not to be asked lightly.

A word no Indian language that I know has (and I wonder if it is nearly obsolete in our language) is endurance. Each time I read through the New Testament I am surprised at how often it occurs. "Sheer dogged endurance" is a phrase in Phillips' translation of I Thessalonians 1:3. Paul endured an astounding variety of trials. Jesus endured the Cross—and the accounts of what happened that awful day are simple and stark: "There they crucified him."

But the idea of endurance in the Bible is associated with some wonderful words, too, I found. Words like faith, patience, crown of life, hope, love, courage. This is what it's about. The emphasis is on the ultimate object, not on how the sufferer actually felt in the middle of the night.

"Who for the joy that was set before him endured the Cross. . . ."

Perhaps we can learn, as we grow, to pay less attention to ourselves and how a thing affects *us*.

"*He* hath borne our griefs."

That ought to be enough.

One of Those
Nineteenth Century Missionaries

"ALL GENERALIZATIONS are false, including this one," yet we keep making them. We create images—graven ones that can't be changed; we dismiss or accept people, products, programs and propaganda according to the labels they come under; we know a little about something, and we treat it as though we know everything.

I couldn't count the times I've heard nineteenth century missions and missionaries cited as examples of stupidity and failure. I heard a whole lecture predicated on this assumption. They were bigoted and imperialistic and naive and arrogant and hypocritical. Some of them probably were some of those things. Some twentieth century missionaries might make the ones of the last century look like paragons by comparison. Missionaries are (and need we go over this again?) human like everybody else, but the world has seen some great ones, some men and women who saw something to which they witnessed with truthfulness and often with real sacrifice.

In that box of old family papers which I mentioned earlier, I found a little frayed booklet put out in 1906 by the Yale Foreign Missionary Society entitled *A Modern Knight,* by Joseph Hopkins Twichell. It broke up some of my categories. It was the story of John Coleridge Patteson, Missionary Bishop of Melanesia.

He was English ("of course," I said to myself—I think of nineteenth century missionaries as English—my generalizations).

He came from a refined English home. He was the nephew of the famous poet Coleridge and the son of an eminent jurist. He had his place "by birth," the booklet says, "in the upper circles of English society." Exactly. No categories shaken by those facts. He grew up in a "praying household, notably pervaded with the spirit of humble piety and with all sweet gospel savors. There is no mistaking the evangelical tone and quality of the religion there prevailing." He went to Eton, was confirmed in the Church of England, and graduated from Oxford, a "rarely accomplished scholar." He was elected fellow of one of the colleges of his university.

But instead of becoming a jurist like his father, John went as a missionary to the Melanesian Islands to work with people who were nearly all savages and naked and cannibalistic—a people marked by "features of repulsiveness and horrible ferocity," according to the chronicler. But it is interesting to note that Patteson himself spoke of them as *men*. To him they were "naturally gentlemanly and well-bred and courteous." "I never saw a 'gent' [by which term I think Patteson meant one who vulgarly tries to imitate a gentleman] in Melanesia, though not a few savages. I vastly prefer the savages."

He saw that they spoke a language, not the "uncouth jargon of barbarians" as many assumed. ("They don't speak a language, do they?" people have asked me of Ecuadorian Indians. "They only make sounds.") Patteson considered some of the Melanesian languages better than English for translating the biblical Hebrew and Greek.

"He gave them his company," writes Twichell. "For years together he scarcely saw any human being save his handful of assistants and his dark-skinned Mel-

152

anesians. He never married. He adopted that wild race as his family." It is Twichell who thinks of them as a wild race. Patteson "had none of the conventional talk about degraded heathen. They were brethren."

He was ecumenical in spirit, at one time having to assume charge of a mission of another denomination where he scrupulously conformed to the practices of that mission, though he admitted that he greatly missed the Prayer Book.

The nurture of the indigenous church has been thought to be a recent emphasis in missionary work. Patteson made this his primary object. He visited the islands for four to six months of each year, and spent the rest of the time instructing people of both sexes at a central location. He insisted that they return to their homes at the end of the instruction period as a test of their own progress.

Patteson himself was up against gross misconceptions of the nature of his work, but he wrote truthfully about it. "In these introductory visits scarcely anything is done or said that resembles mission work in stories. The crowd is great, the noise greater. The heat, the dirt, the inquisitiveness, the begging, make something unlike the interesting pictures in a missionary magazine of an amiable individual very correctly got up in a white tie and black tailed coat, and a group of very attentive, decently clothed, nicely washed natives."

Patteson could not abide sentimentality, that lifeless, heartless and ultimately cruel idol of many Christians. "One who takes a sentimental view of coral islands and coconuts is of course worse than useless," he wrote. "A man possessed with the idea that he is making a sacrifice will never do. A man who thinks any kind of work beneath him will simply be in the way." He was to be found milking cows and cutting out girls' dresses and doing things the people in England thought shocking.

"Integration" was not a word in his vocabulary as we use it today, and he deplored "that pride of race which prompts a white man to regard colored people as inferior to himself. They (the natives) have a strong sense of, and acquiescence in, their inferiority ('Does an ant know how to speak to a cow?' one of them once said) but if we treat them as inferiors they will always remain in that position."

Progress reports? "My objection to mission *reports* has always been that the readers want to hear of progress, and the writers are thus tempted to write of it; and may they not, without knowing it, be, at times, hasty that they may seem to be progressing? People expect too much. Because missionary work looks like failure, it does not follow that it is. Our Savior's work looked like a failure. He made no mistakes either in what He taught or in the way of teaching it, and He succeeded, though not to the eyes of men."

Patteson saw his own work as seed sowing. He was prepared to wait long and patiently and not to dig up in doubt what he had planted in faith. He gave to the handful of Melanesians whom he was training a care of instruction and discipline that was "deliberate and painstaking beyond measure."

We have heard missionaries of the last century accused of transferring European civilization to the native culture as though it were synonymous with Christianity. Patteson said, "I have long felt that there is almost harm done in trying to make these islanders like English people. They are to be Melanesian, not English, Christians. . . . Unless we can denationalize ourselves, and eliminate all that belongs to us as English and not as Christians, we cannot be to them what a well instructed countryman of theirs may be. . . . Christianity is the religion of humanity at large. It has room for all. It takes in all shades and diversities of character, race, etc."

When he was little over 40, Patteson visited an island he had never been to. He was received from his ship in a native canoe and taken to shore. The crew waited hours for his return, and at last saw two canoes leaving the beach, one towing the other which appeared to be empty. Soon the empty canoe was cast adrift while the other was paddled rapidly back to shore. Cautiously the boat's crew made toward the drifting canoe. As they drew alongside they saw the body of John Coleridge Patteson, wrapped in a mat, a palm frond laid on his chest. It was the year 1871.

The church, for the most part, has forgotten this name in the long list of its martyrs. It forgets most of what has been done and suffered, and thinks it is doing and suffering now as never before. We boast of our progress (from missions to "mission," for example) and criticize those bunglers of 100 years ago. But criticism is an easy chair exercise, especially when the critic does not trouble himself to look at the data but relies chiefly on what he himself feels or on "what everybody knows"—on generalizations.

Thank heaven the work of Patteson and all other missionaries, as well as the work you and I have to do today, is subject to the judgment of "a judge who is God of all," who never mistakes the counterfeit for the real, never needs to revise his categories, never lumps men together.

What About the Aucas?

YESTERDAY I SAW some film footage of a man in boots and parka walking along a beach. The beach looked empty and very cold. When the sound track told me that he was on the northern side of Alaska, I knew that it must be very cold indeed, but the beach was not as empty as it looked. He began picking up things—an old tennis shoe, a soda can, a tuna fish can, a piece of tire tread, a plastic cup. The pitch was, of course, ecology. We've polluted everything in our forty-eight older states (a bumper sticker says "Lake Erie died for your sins") and have gone a long way toward polluting the two newest ones. But we haven't by any means stopped there. It's not only our own beaches and lakes and the poisoned fish and oil-slicked waterfowl and detergent-fluffed rivers and thickened air that I worry about. Our civilization relentlessly elbows its way into oceans and deserts and jungles that don't belong to us at all.

I had a letter from Ecuador describing what is happening among the Auca Indians.

The oil companies have moved in. There are camps and airstrips and white men all over the place. Aucas who had isolated themselves even from the rest of the tribe have been pried loose from their hiding places. I read of helicopters flying in and out at the request of Auca Indians who have been furnished with short-wave radios. They call in asking for medicines (meningitis was a threat—where did it come from?), for cloth, pots, machetes, beads, cotton thread, flashlight batteries and replacement parts for their new cassette tape recorders. One of them wanted a cap (a baseball cap? a golf or hunting cap? I have no idea) as a reward for an airstrip which he said he had built all by himself. Some have been given cookies and taken for rides in helicopters, and of course this means there is a certain amount of jockeying for places on the flights. Brand new tensions have been created over who gets what and when. One man managed to get himself a second wife (he still has the first) as a result of improved relations with the "downriver" group.

My head spins as I read all of this. Back in 1958 when Rachel Saint, my small daughter and I went to live with the Aucas they were virtually a Stone Age people. (A lot of excitement was engendered last year when someone discovered a Stone Age tribe in the Philippines. You would have thought no one in this century had ever heard of such a thing, but my guess is that Amazonia probably has a dozen or more tribes no one has turned up yet.) The Aucas had kept themselves so aloof from everybody else, including other Indians, that most of them had never seen anybody they didn't know. Repeat: *never seen anybody they didn't know*. They lived by hunting and planting and gathering. They knew how to make baskets and clay pots and palmwood spears and blowguns and fiber hammocks. And, occasionally, they killed people.

Nearly sixteen years have passed. Rachel Saint has stayed with them most of that time, has taught some of them to read and write, and is translating the Bible into their language. But even in the two short years that I lived there, there were tremendous changes. Most of them started to wear clothes, and when I had the Quichua Indians come to build me a four-walled house, so that my daughter would have a place to do her correspondence school work, the Aucas built some

157

four-walled houses, too. They wanted screened windows like mine and they asked me for hammers and nails. They quit using firesticks the minute they understood what a match could do. Aluminum pots obviously were easy to get and lasted forever, so their fragile, heavy clay pots went. Hair was cut, earplugs were out, glass beads were in. Later on there was a polio epidemic, presumably a gift of civilization, which took the lives of a score or more and left others crippled.

Now I am trying to picture them manning shortwave radios, giving injections of medicines they have received by helicopter, airplane or parachute, taping things on cassettes, and a man named Monca giving "an intensive orientation course concerning the advancing petroleum companies." Monca himself can have only the dimmest understanding of what it's all about, but he's trying his best to get the others to be nice to the invaders, for in his mind it's all tied up with the Word of God which was what the first foreigners brought. The petroleum companies on their part are being very obliging. Anything that keeps the Aucas healthy and happy and out of the way is a small price to pay for what they're after. Years ago one company had braved the savages and staked out some claims but withdrew when a number of employees were speared.

But now the Aucas are tamed. They have learned that outsiders are not cannibals after all—not exactly. They have had it carefully explained that what the *kuwuri* (foreigners) want is something the Auca doesn't want and didn't even know was there. The missionaries, perhaps reluctantly, seem to be cooperating with the businessmen, although they have tried to see that the government officially designates a portion of the rich rain forest as Auca territory. But can anybody explain to the Aucas that their days are numbered and that they won't be of any use to the *kuwuri* after a while?

To us it's a familiar pattern. It sounds distressingly like a rerun of North American history. The Indians such as the Iroquois in our country who were not congenial and reasonable folk made it a little harder and slower for the civilized folks. But the Aucas, satisfied that we aren't really going to eat them, have been wonderful about it all. They were touchingly anxious to do whatever they thought we wanted. They didn't like scenes, and I saw how quickly they would conform in order to avoid them. It is not hard to get them to make adjustments—they put up with me and all my peculiarities with great good humor and good will. Two of them went willingly to West Berlin with Rachel a few years ago to tell a large convention how they had become Christians. Three of them last year appeared on the *Today* show to explain that they now believe in God.

And that is exactly the reason (to answer the question so often put to missionaries, "Why don't you leave them alone?") that we went in there in the first place—to tell them the good news about God.

The anthropologist feels that he alone has the right to breach the privacy of a primitive tribe, for he doesn't want to change a thing. He does change things, though, willy-nilly. His presence is like the grain of sand in an oyster. It sets up an irritation. So does the missionary. He, suspicious of and deplored by the anthropologist, goes in meaning to change things, for Christ makes all things new. But he does not want necessarily to pave the way for capitalism.

Capitalism follows, and the changes are radical, rapid and implacable.

People are relieved to hear of certain changes and outraged to hear of others. We love to think there are some Edens left in the world to which no Get-Away flights have yet been scheduled by the airlines. People

159

like to look at pictures of people in their "before" state. (Yes, I, like everybody else, have thousands of slides I wish I could *induce* somebody to look at, but the ones of the Aucas people sometimes *ask* to see.) But faces fall when changes are mentioned because there are sure to be some of the wrong kind. Is there a way to keep our grubby hands off what we don't want to change?

Does the Auca for whom we are asked to pray because he is particularly "resistant to the Gospel" actually have a premonition of the disaster about to overtake his tribe? Pontiac and Tecumseh were tough men to deal with, too. We look at their noble profiles now and want to cry.

Christians are meant to be messengers of the kingdom of heaven. That kingdom brings change, but it is likened to leaven and to seed, things which work in very slow and secret ways. The questions raised by our attempts to bear the message and our mistakes and false moves are very hard ones. Only God knows which of us have responded to his call in faith, and this will determine our response to that fearful-hopeful promise of Matthew 13, "The Son of Man will send out his angels and they will uproot from the kingdom everything that is spoiling it and all those who live in defiance of its laws, and will throw them into the blazing furnace."

Women in World Missions

ABOUT FOUTEEN years ago I had the great good fortune to meet an unforgettable character whose biography is entitled *The Small Woman,* and whose life story was told, after a fashion, in a movie called "The Inn of the Sixth Happiness." She was Gladys Aylward. To hear this little creature of four feet eleven inches, dressed as a Chinese, tell her own story in a stentorian voice was a stunning experience. I remember how she took the microphone and with no preliminary nonsense whatever thundered forth, "I should like to read just one verse. 'And Jehovah God spoke to Abram and he said, "Get out!" ' " She told us the story of Abraham's faith and his move into an unknown land. Then she said, "And one day, in a little flat in London, Jehovah God spoke to a Cockney parlor maid and he said, 'Get out!' 'Where do you want me to go Lord?' I said, and he said, 'To China.' " So Gladys Aylward went to China. And what a story that was—a train across Europe and Russia, a frying pan strapped to the outside of her suitcase, an angel's guidance in the dead of night onto a forbidden ship, a breath-taking saga of one woman's obedience to the call of God.

Some twenty-six centuries earlier the word of the Lord came to a much more likely prospect than a parlor maid—he was the descendant of priests—and in a much more likely place than the city of London, Anathoth in the land of Benjamin. Isn't it easier to believe that the word of the Lord might come to somebody in Anathoth than in London? Or in Urbana? The man was Jeremiah, appointed a prophet of the nations, but he was reluctant to accept the appointment. "Ah, Lord God," he groaned, "Behold, I do not know how to speak for I am only a youth." But the Lord said to him, "Do not say 'I am only a youth,' for to all to whom I send you you shall go, and whatever I command you you shall speak. Be not afraid of them, for I am with you."

God's call frequently brings surprise and dismay, and a protest that one is not qualified. Jeremiah hoped he might get out of it by reminding Almighty God (in case Almighty God had not noticed) that he was too young. Gladys Aylward did not strike me as timid, but she might have called God's attention to her limitations: she too was young; she was poor; she had no education; she was no good at anything but dusting and she was a *woman*. In the case of both prophet and parlor maid, however, the issue at stake was identical. The issue was obedience. Questions of intellect and experience, of age and sex, were quite beside the point. God said *do this* and they did it.

What is the place of women in world missions? Jesus said, "You (and the word means all of you, male and female) are my witnesses. *You* are the salt of the earth. *You* are the light of the world." And there have been countless thousands who, without reference to where they came from or what they knew or who they were, have believed that Jesus meant what he said and have set themselves to follow.

Today strident female voices are raised to remind us, shrilly and *ad nauseam,* that women are equal with men. But such a question has never even arisen in connection with the history of Christian missions. In fact, for many years, far from being excluded, women constituted the majority among foreign missionaries.

"Missionary," of course, is a term which does not

occur in the Bible. I like the word witness, and it is a good, biblical word meaning someone who has seen something. The virgin Mary saw an angel and heard his word and committed herself irretrievably when she said, "Behold the handmaid of the Lord." This decision meant sacrifice—the giving up of her reputation and, for all she knew then, of her marriage and her own cherished plans. "Be it unto me according to thy word." She knew the word was from God, and she put her life on the line because of it. The thing God was asking her to do, let us not forget, was a thing that only a woman could do.

The early history of the church mentions other women who witnessed—by ministering to Christ during his earthly work, cooking for him, probably, making a bed, poviding clothes and washing them—women who were willing and glad to do whatever he needed to have done. (And some of you who despise that sort of work—would you do it if it was for him? "Inasmuch as ye have done it unto one of the least of these my brethren," Jesus said, "ye have done it unto me.") There was Priscilla, coadjutor of the apostle Paul. There was a business woman named Lydia who opened her heart to what was said and then opened her home to those who said it. There must have been thousands of women like these who did what lay in their power to do because with all their hearts they wanted to do it. They had seen something; they had heard a word; they knew their responsibility.

In the conversion of the Teutonic peoples, women played an important role. Clovis, King of the Franks in the fifth century, made this mistake of marrying a Christian princess, Clotilda from Burgundy, and through her was eventually baptized. According to the Venerable Bede's account, King Ethelbert of Kent made the same mistake in the next century, and his queen, Bertha, persuaded him to allow a monk named Augustine to settle in Canterbury. Within a year ten thousand Saxons were converted.

One of the earliest of those who were actually called missionaries was Gertrude Ras Egede, a Danish woman. Although violently opposed to her husband's going to Greenland to try to find the remnants of the church which had been lost for several centuries, she soon saw that her opposition to him was in reality opposition to God. She repented and went with her husband to what turned out to be a far cry from the "Green Land" they had expected. It was a frigid Godforsaken wasteland, where Gertrude Ras Egede died after fifteen years of hard work—generally called "labor" if a missionary does it. (We all know that missionaries don't go, they "go forth," they don't walk, they "tread the burning sands," they don't die, they "lay down their lives." But the work gets done even if it is sentimentalized!)

Women in the United States began to swing into action for the cause of world missions in the beginning of the nineteenth century. There was a Boston Female Society for Missionary Purposes founded in 1800, and a Miss Mary Well founded what was called the Cent Society in 1802 "for females who are disposed to contribute their mite towards so noble a design as diffusion of the gospel light among the shades of darkness and superstition." There was a Fuel Society which paid for coal for young seminarians, a Boston Fragment Society which provided clothes for indigent mothers and their babies. Massachusetts and Connecticut swarmed with what were called "female missionary societies" by 1812, and by 1816 three Baptist wives, supported by these societies, were en route to Ceylon as missionaries. "If not deceived in our motives," one of them wrote, "we have been induced to leave our beloved friends and native shores to cross the tempestuous deep, from love to Christ and the souls which he died to purchase. And now we are ready, waiting with the humble hope of being employed, in his own time and way, in building up his kingdom."

I was surprised to learn that the Civil War strongly affected the progress of women in missions. It was an educative force in America, for through it women were driven to organize because of their pity for the fighting men and their patriotism. In the ten years following the war, scores of organizations, including many new missionary societies, were launched.

The nineteenth century mind boggled at the thought of single women serving on a foreign field. A few widows were accepted, having supposedly profited by the guidance of husbands and therefore being more knowledgeable and dependable than single women could be expected to be. The first single woman on record who was sent to a foreign land was one Betsy Stockton and she was black.

Of Eleanor Macomber of Burma it was said, "No husband helped her decide the momentous question, and when she resolved, it was to go *alone*. With none to share her thousand cares and complexities, with no heart to keep time with the wild beatings of her own, she, a friendless woman, crossed the deep dark ocean, and on soil never trodden by the feet of Christian men, erected the banner of the Cross." This is typical of the sentimental view of missionaries which makes most of us cringe. This description was written by a man, but don't let his phrases "weak, defenseless woman," and "the wild beatings of her heart" blur the single fact of Eleanor Macomber's action. Don't stay home because you don't like the *image*. True faith is action. Faith cometh by hearing, and results in *doing*.

I could go on listing what women have done to prove that they have had an important role in world missions. There were Mary Slessor of Calabar, Lottie Moon of

China, Amy Carmichael of India, Rosalind Goforth of China, Malla Moe of Africa—of whom it was said that although she could not preach like Peter nor pray like Paul told thousands of the love of Jesus. And besides these names there have surely been tens of thousands of nameless nuns and other anonymous women who have done what God sent them to do—and they've done it without the tub-thumping of modern egalitarian movements. They had a place and they knew they had it because Scripture says they have.

You read in your Bible from Romans 12, "All members do not have the same function." There is nothing interchangeable about the sexes, and there is nothing interchangeable about Christians. God has given gifts that *differ*. They differ *according to the grace given to us*. You and I, whether we are men or women, have nothing to do with the choice of the gift. We have everything to do with the use of the gift.

There are diversities of operations, but the same Spirit. There are varieties of personalities but all are made in the image of God. As a woman I find clear guidance in Scripture about my position in church and home. I find no exemption from the obligations of commitment and obedience. My obligations have certainly varied from time to time and from place to place. I started my missionary work as a single woman with three other single women. There was no church, there were no believers and there were no male missionaries. Later I was a wife and had to rearrange certain priorities in accordance with what I understood to be my job, as a wife, as a co-worker with my husband in the field and later as a mother.

When my husband was killed by Indians, I found myself in some indefinable positions. There wasn't one missionary man left in Ecuador at that time who spoke the jungle Quichua language. There was no one to teach the young Quichua Christians, no one to lead the church, no one but women to carry on where five missionary men had left off. The door to the Auca tribe had slammed shut for those men and was, to our astonishment, opened to two women. It didn't look to me like a woman's job but God's categories are not always ours. I had to shuffle my categories many times during my last eight years of missionary work. Since coming back to the States I've had a career of sorts, I've been a wife and a housewife once more, and again I'm a widow.

But it is the same faithful Lord who calls me by name and never loses track of my goings and reminds us all in a still, small voice, "Ye are my witnesses that ye might know and believe me and understand that I am he." There's our primary responsibility; to *know him*. I can't be a witness unless I've seen something, unless I know what it is I am to testify to.

And it is the Lord of the universe who calls you—women and men—and offers you today a place in his program. Your education or lack of it, your tastes and prejudices and fears and ambitions, your age or sex or color or height or marital status or income bracket are all things which may be offered to God, after you've presented your bodies as a living sacrifice. And God knows exactly what to do with them. They're not obstacles if you hand them over. Be still and know that he is God. Sit in silence and wonder and expectancy and never doubt that the Lord of your life has his own way of getting through to you to let you know the specifics of his will.

And if you know that you've seen something, you can add your voice to the host of witnesses like G. K. Chesterton who, in answer to the historical query of why Christianity was accepted, answers for millions of others: "Because it fits the lock; because it is like life.

We are Christians not because we worship a key but because we have passed a door and felt the wind that is the trumpet of liberty blow over the land of the living."

A Modern Pastoral

"THE CARE of sheep is the care of the weak. The strong will take care of themselves." It was Mari, the shepherd's wife, who was explaining things to me as we walked from the farmhouse to the pens where the rams were to be dipped that day.

The farm, Brynuchaf, lies on a steep hillside in a remote part of Wales, not far from Aran, one of the highest mountains. There are mountains on all sides, separated by deep ravines and green valleys. John's sheep graze on the sides of two mountains. As I looked out the window of the farmhouse earlier that morning I had seen him on his horse coming across the meadow in the mist with the rams, his dog Mack circling at top speed around the flock, keeping them together, urging them along at his master's command. Cows shared the meadow as well, but they chewed serenely, ignoring the sheep, the shepherd and his horse and dog, conscious that nothing was asked of them this time.

I was visiting the farm only for a night, and John and Mari tried to pack as much into the time as they could. They had met me in the little town of Machynlleth and driven me up what seemed to me impossibly narrow roads to the farm which lay nearly hidden behind a row of lime trees. After an excellent dinner of their own roast lamb Mari and I had put on rubber boots ("Wellingtons," she called them) and gone up through a lovely pasture to a ravine where there was a great cataract: In order to reach a spot where we could see it we had to clamber over a fence and down a steep pathway, holding onto branches and roots as we went. When we reached a ledge where we could stand we saw the waterfall, pouring over the huge rock walls, leaping from pool to pool, runnning at last in clearest crystal below. As we stood in the dim filtered light of the forest Mari took from the top of her Wellington a piece of paper from which she read to me what she had written about the scene before us. She saw the waterfall as a visible sign of invisible verities—the total giving of itself as it poured itself out over the rocks, the "leap of faith" from pool to pool, the purification which finally resulted.

Before we climbed back up again she pointed out to me initials elegantly carved in the living face of the rock by the ledge on which we stood—*J.D.E. 1736, W.W. 1729* and others. My imagination was kindled at once. Others had known this secret dell, had stood where we stood, had wanted it to be known that they had stood here.

After tea Mari drove me north through the highest pass in Wales, Bwlch-y-Groes. She pointed to a place on the road where long ago robbers had lain in wait for a traveling preacher known to be carrying a sum of money from one church to another. The preacher had been joined just before he reached this place by a man on a white horse who, when greeted, did not reply. The two rode on together in silence, and the robbers, seeing the preacher accompanied, kept to their hiding place, their plans foiled. The man on the white horse vanished a little way beyond, and it was then that the preacher knew that an angel had been given charge over him, to keep him in all his ways.

As we drove down the other side of the pass Mari told me about Mary Jones, a girl who saved her ha'pennies for months in order to buy a Bible. When she had enough she took her shoes in her hand and walked barefoot (for she could not afford to wear out her shoes) many miles to the town of Bala where she knocked on the door of the man who sold Bibles, Thomas Charles. Ah, but there were none left for sale, he told her. Mary Jones stood on the doorstep and wept. But when she had told her story, Thomas Charles gave her a Bible of his own, and resolved then and there that those who wanted Bibles should have them. It was thus that the British and Foreign Bible Society was founded. His motto, a marvel of alliteration in Welsh, was *Beible i bawd a bobl y byd*— "Bibles for all of the people of the world." When we reached the village of Bala, Mari showed me the plaque over the door of the house where Mary Jones wept.

Late in the evening John and Mari sang for me, standing in their living room by the piano as I played some of the great Welsh hymns whose tunes have long been familiar to me. They sang in Welsh, of course, a beautiful rich and rolling language meant for singing.

Before we went to bed they promised that I should see the sheep dogs in operation next morning.

The rams were brought into a pen near the sheep dip, and Mack, the Scottish collie, raced around through the pasture to take up his position on the other side of the gate through which the rams were to be sent. He crouched in what I learned is the characteristic sheep dog posture, all alertness, intensity, attention, his eyes blazing as he waited for his master to open the gate.

John seized a ram by the curled horns, set him back on his haunches while he inspected the hoofs, shaved the hoofs a little with a small sharp knife because of a disease which causes the sheep to limp, and then hurled the ram straight into the dip. The poor creature plunged in with a great splash, struggled to climb out the side. Mack went into action, snapping at the ram's

171

head to send him back into the milky, strong-smelling fluid. Just as the ram reached the far end the shepherd caught him by the horns with a wooden implement a little like a hoe, spun him around, pulled him back and dunked him completely under, eyes, nose, ears, and all. He held the ram for a second or two, then allowed him to struggle away and out of the pool, spluttering and shaking his head, shaking his heavy wool coat, amazed at the treatment he had received. Yet he opened not his mouth.

If only, I was thinking, if only there were some way to explain to the sheep why his trusted shepherd treats him so. But there is no possible way to explain. Such knowledge is too wonderful for him; he cannot attain it.

When all the rams had been dipped John rode out on his horse again, calling Mack to the pasture where there were forty or fifty ewes. Here the dog crouched facing the sheep, listening for the shepherd's whistle. The whistle was his command, and he understood exactly what he was to do. He circled to the right, circled to the left, herding the frightened sheep together, moving them according to his master's instructions, given only with the little metal whistle.

"The sheep haven't a clue what's happening, have they?" I asked.

"Not a clue," said Mari.

The dog never took his eyes from his work. No matter what the command he watched the sheep. But his ears were in tune every second with the whistle. At times he raced like the wind in obedience to the command, and when the command came to stop, he put on four-wheel brakes. Instantly he came to a halt, always listening, always facing the sheep, not asking why he should be told to stop.

"The dog doesn't understand the pattern," Mari said, "only obedience."

What the dog can not see the shepherd saw—the weak ewe that lagged behind, the one caught in a bush, the danger that lay ahead for the flock. But the shepherd's will was the dog's joy. It was obvious. Mack knew sheep through and through. He was made to herd sheep. He loved the work. But he loved his master most. "I delight to do thy will, yea, thy law is within my heart" was what his every movement proclaimed.

And the shepherd loved the sheep. "John loves to be with them," Mari said. "They are his life."

The good shepherd gives his life for the sheep.

I traveled that same afternoon by train to England, musing on the fact that it took a jumbo jet, a bus, a train and a car to get me to that mountain fastness where a few truths that are changeless were known to me again, and words that I knew by heart sprang up to teach me by living illustrations.